PRAISE FOR WIS

"In a season when so many are asking deep questions of meaning for their life and faith, it is a good time to revisit the wisdom of Ecclesiastes. In *Wisdom for Old Souls*, Dave Booram shares his own honest conversation with this ancient, bracing book. I urge all old souls, those with few years or those with more, to read, reflect and find hope and encouragement in these pages. "

Alan Fadling, President & Founder, Unhurried Living and Author of "A Year of Slowing Down"

"This is a book for people who ask questions about themselves, about God and about life. The Bible reminds us to "Let the Spirit change your way of thinking" (Ephesians 4:23 CEV). This book invites us to join with David Booram as he asks questions and allows the Spirit to change his own way of thinking. It is a treasure to be savored in God's presence."

Alice Fryling, Author of "Aging Faithfully: The Holy Invitation of Growing Older"

"In *Wisdom for Old Souls*, Dave Booram guides you through the deeply personal process of coming to understand the new landscape for meaning that emerges in the second half of life. Through a creative dialogue with the author of Ecclesiastes, this book points the reader beyond the "vanities" of life to the humble and hidden places of substance and God's ever-working presence."

Steven Lawson, Founder, Monk Manual

"In a day in which wisdom can seem to be in short supply all around us, it is the very thing you'll find on every page of *Wisdom for Old Souls*. In the 100 meditations rooted simultaneously in the Book of Ecclesiastes and in David Booram's reflective Christian spirituality, you will find hope and wise guidance for every season of your life."

Jeff Crosby, Author of "The Language of the Soul"

"Dave Booram invites readers into a hundred-day conversation with the Preacher who scribed the book of Ecclesiastes, with God, with ourselves, and with the world in which we live. This shimmering guided meditation calls us into the kind of unvarnished honesty that is the soil in which both humility and wisdom grows."

Michelle Van Loon, Author of "Translating Your Past: Finding Meaning in Family Ancestry, Genetic Clues, and Generational Trauma"

"From the outset of this extraordinary volume, Dave Booram asks a question that awakens me: Can there be a different center to my life than work? I didn't know it until I read it, but this is a question I want to live into! With deep insight and creativity, Dave weaves us through Ecclesiastes in a fresh way giving us 100 days to grow in wisdom—a gift we should all give ourselves. You'll want to linger with, hover over, and savor these words for Old Souls, so that you, too, like Dave Booram, might become one."

Carolyn Carney, National Director of Spiritual Formation, InterVarsity Christian Fellowship

"Dave Booram harvests the riches of decades of deep and vulnerable practice in Ignatian prayer to give us a devotional that isn't just a collection of heart-warming sentiments. Each entry in *Wisdom for Old Souls* is a verdant opportunity to discover anew how God is present and at work in every season of our lives."

Ben Sternke, Pastor, Leadership Coach and Co-Author of "Having the Mind of Christ"

"Ecclesiastes is wisdom for us, but sometimes hard to access. Dave has written an extended meditation that does what sermons and commentaries can't: it invites us to inhabit and submerge our lives in Scripture, slowly drinking in the words of God and learning to talk with him. Offering just enough structure and guidance to get us going, Dave creates space in the beauty of Ecclesiastes for us to meet with God and receive goodness; take your time and let your soul soak up wisdom as you work your way through this one."

Matt Tebbe, Co-Planter of The Table and Co-Founder of Gravity Leadership

"With the wisdom of a seasoned spiritual director, Dave Booram opens space for old souls (like me) to reflect, question and listen as we journey into the last third of life. In *Wisdom for Old Souls: Ecclesiastes Transposed from the Voice of the Eternal*, Dave invites us to listen in on his conversations with God, bringing us the wisdom and wonderings of Ecclesiastes. For all of us sensing an invitation to re-center our days and re-orient our lives for a new, later-in-life season, this collection of readings and prompts serves as a kind and faithful companion."

Susan Carson, Author, Podcaster and Executive Director of Roots&Branches Network

"Reading the collected wisdom in this timely book is second only to sitting across from David Booram at his home in Indianapolis as we settle into a time of deep, soulful listening together. In these pages, just as in Dave's presence, one can't help but open up to God's loving voice within. I'm grateful for Dave's "holy audacity" in the following one-hundred colloquies. David Booram has walked the humble and hard road with Jesus over the course of his life. Now, his enduring gift to us is a well-worn witness to the heart of God for young and old souls alike. May each person who picks up *Wisdom for Old Souls* accept the invitation to a slow journey, not as a casual observer, but as a beloved participant in a sacred conversation which will continue from here into eternity."

Adam Ormord, Executive Director of Grafted Life Ministries and ESDA

"David has written out of his own journey, his own questions what is true for many of us in our journeys and our questions. It begs us to pay attention. How are we in the world and not of it? Who can we have a conversation with about what seems to be adrift in us and in the world? This book, *Wisdom for Old Souls*, invites... the three in one God to address us in the shadow places of our lives in the spirit of grace and truth. It is a fresh way of coming home to ourselves, to God and to one another. I am going to take this journey. Thank you, David. This is good wisdom for today!"

Sibyl Towner, Co-Director of The Springs Retreat Center and Co-Author of "Listen to My Life"

"There is a grace in being known in our questions and being responded to in our confusions —a possibility only through long relationship. Dave Booram's *Wisdom for Old Souls* invites readers into that relationship—opening a vulnerable window into his conversations with God and modeling a way for readers to engage God in the complexity, wrestling, and doubts of our own lives. Booram offers himself as an icon, an open door, and so allows others to truly encounter the One who longs to call you "old friend.""

Tara Owens, CSD, CSDS, Executive Director of Anam Cara Ministries

WISDOM
FOR OLD SOULS

WISDOM
FOR OLD SOULS

Ecclesiastes Transposed from
the Voice of the Eternal

DAVID BOORAM

Fall Creek
Abbey Press

Indianapolis, Indiana

Cover design and interior design by Emma C. Hogsett

Printed by Gorham Printing, Inc., in the United States of America

First printing January 2023

ISBN Softcover: 978-1-7374769-1-7

Published by Fall Creek Abbey Press
2439 N. Park Ave.
Indianapolis, IN 46205

www.FallCreekAbbey.org

For my dad, David Lewis Booram,
and my oldest granddaughter, Harper Lillian Booram—
two of God's lovely souls whose lives, filled with joys and sorrows,
have added vivid poignancy to the words of this book.

"Personal answers to ultimate questions.
That is what we seek."
Alexander Eliot

A WORK CENTERED LIFE

I started this writing project a few months before my 66th birthday. Beth and I were feeling bleary-eyed having recently brought our new puppy home and having our empty-nest years interrupted by this energetic newborn. To cope, we tag-teamed caring for Flo and traded off the morning and afternoon, so that each of us could have a small, overdue personal retreat. As I settled into my time, I did an inventory of my life, noticing the givens of my life, the conditions of my body, that which was occupying my mind, my prevalent emotions, and my unanswered questions and longings. It's a simple practice that I've used for several years now to check in with myself as I begin my retreats. As I reviewed what I'd written, I started to notice a theme. Some phrases that stood out to me were:

- ❖ I'll be eligible for Social Security next year
- ❖ I feel tired
- ❖ I'd like to work less and play more
- ❖ What do You want from me in "retirement?"

Reflecting on these statements I found myself writing the following:

> *"I'm aware of a certain prejudice we seem to have toward the word/vision/notion of retirement. But I am getting tired of centering life around work/ministry. Could there be a different center to life in which work is only a part? And if so, what might that center be?"*

A different center than work? Unchallenged, have you noticed how work becomes the default focus of most of our time and energy, forcing the other aspects of our human experience into the shadowy margins of our hours and days to feed on the scraps and fend for themselves? Later that afternoon, as I attempted to listen to God's voice, I sensed the following:

> *"David, you have not only My permission, you have My blessing to re-center your days, to re-orient your priorities away from work's primacy and toward the richness of this season, your life's full flowering! How do you imagine this looking in practice?"*

This is the question I have been pondering for the past few months. If work is not the center, what is? What do I want it to be? What does God want it to be? I've not come up with a simple, clear answer yet. But in the midst of my retreat day as I sought some fresh perspective, I was drawn to read through the book of

Ecclesiastes. I wondered if this strangely evocative little book (which has always seemed like an outlier in the canon of scripture), might just contain what I needed to navigate my last-third-of-life questions. I sensed that what I was seeking might become clearer to me in the wide-angled, glaring perspective of this work's honesty and angst.

As the next few months rolled by, little did I know what the new year would bring to me and my family. It began in March when my mom at 87 broke her hip and needed a total hip replacement. As an only child, it fell on me to care for her along with the growing needs of my 90-year-old dad, who was living alone. The weight of their decline burrowed its way from the margins to center stage of my life. Then in April our nine-year-old granddaughter was shockingly diagnosed with leukemia. The emotional upheaval of Harper's journey with cancer is still heavy on our minds and hearts from the beginning to the end of each day. Finally, in June, my dad fell, developed an infection that became septic and led to a series of cardiac episodes. After 3 weeks in the hospital and rehab he died. Losing him has affected me more than I imagined. His absence has set in motion new feelings and questions.

Not long after these events, I noticed that I was unusually low. My thoughts were rather morose, even despairing. Questions like these seemed to circle around me like buzzards searching for carrion:

- What does it matter?
- Why do I care about this?
- Why work so hard when nothing really changes?
- What would happen (or not) if I just gave up?
- Is the world (or anything else) better off in any significant way because of me?
- Why am I still here?
- What still moves me?
- What interests me? What captures my heart — of what am I wholehearted?

I told Beth a few days later that "I just don't feel like myself." Something has shifted in me and I'm not sure what it is. Am "I" gone? Is the "self" I once was beyond me now, or rather behind me? Is it being replaced or transformed into I know not what? Am I waiting for the "new me" or the "next me"? I simply don't know. And so, it's from these colliding points of view, my nearing old age, and my experience of these life altering losses that I eventually picked up my pen to capture this Divine transposition of Ecclesiastes.

A VENTRILOQUIST'S CRAFT

I have a friend who is a professional ventriloquist. I've watched him countless times "throw his voice" and in so doing, entertain children and adults alike as they are drawn to see reality from a new vantage point through his creative illusion. Even though we all know it's a practiced craft, when we are taken up in the moment, the character on his lap is no longer simply a "dummy" made of wood. It comes alive!

Most scholars agree that based on linguistic analysis, even though the book of Ecclesiastes claims to have been written from the point of view of a wise and obscenely affluent king of Israel (often attributed to Solomon), it was actually written much later. It simply could not have been written by Solomon or any of his direct heirs. As a work of creative imagination, the human author seems to have "thrown his voice" in a way that takes on the life experience and perspective of the wealthy sage. This artistic technique causes normal people like us to perk up and take notice. Since most of us will never be that well off, surely someone like this will have it all figured out.

To say that it's a creative technique or literary device does not take away from the profound spiritual depth of the book's arguments. In fact, I find it rather enhances them. These are the perennial questions and conundrums that are asked by all generations regardless of social or economic class. Having someone at the top of the food chain wrestle and then be rewarded with such little resolution can be surprisingly consoling to us who find ourselves further down the chain. The book of Ecclesiastes is a form of "shadow wisdom" that starkly challenges the conventional wisdom often dressed up in our religious communities as God's wisdom.

WRITING A COLLOQUY

In *Wisdom for Old Souls*, I am "throwing my voice," so to speak, into a Divine point of view. Technically, it is an exercise in writing a colloquy. A colloquy is a prayer practice cultivated within Ignatian spirituality. Simply put, the word colloquy means conversation. In contrast to a soliloquy, which is a one-sided monologue, a colloquy is mutual and interactive. In prayer, this takes on the form of dialogue, of listening as well as voicing one's questions and opinions.

Wisdom for Old Souls is an extended example of this prayer form. In it I have used the text of Ecclesiastes to form the human side of the colloquy and the writings I've included reflect my listening to the Divine voice.

To what end? Am I actually claiming to "hear" God speaking to me in these exact and specific words? Good question. I view it this way: In recording the dialogue back to me, or in this case, to the author of Ecclesiastes, I am better able to consider how well I am hearing. What's my level of detecting and discerning the heart of God? What do these words reveal about my image of God?

For me, writing a colloquy helps me locate where I am in my spiritual journey. As I read back what I've "heard" from the Divine perspective, I come face to face with what I actually sense is true from my lived, but limited life experience and also what I believe God thinks and feels and is doing in my life, in the world, and in my relationship with it all. In other words, I am given an opportunity, I am given permission, to say what I really think and try it on. We rarely are given the floor by others to share many of these thoughts and beliefs that seem to be quietly milling about in the shadows of our consciousness. We may not even be aware of them ourselves until we take the risk to put them out there by writing them down.

What do I look for as I review my colloquies?

- How loving are the tone and words?
- How hopeful are they?
- Are they overly or hyper-spiritual?
- How friendly are they toward humanity's limits and failings?
- Do they portray a sense of Divine humility?
- Are they seasoned with humor and Divine enjoyment?
- Finally, do they make room for mystery and not knowing?

I'm sure you could come up with your own list. I'd encourage you to name for yourself what gives you a sense that you are hearing from God. The process of creating your own "list of authentication" might be revelatory to you in and of itself. What do you deep down believe about the heart and the values of your Divine Conversation Partner?

I've come to accept that I will make many mistakes in my understanding of who God is and what God values. But I've determined that if I'm going to be mistaken, I know what I want to be mistaken for. Since the scriptures say that the greatest of all virtues is love, and that any and all commandments are summarized by loving God and loving others, I've decided to err on the side of assuming too much of God's love rather than too little. In other words, I've come to stand with those who are unafraid to proclaim the absolute wideness of God's mercy and the irresistible depths of God's understanding of what it means to be human.

HOW TO USE THIS BOOK

The author of Ecclesiastes is to be commended for sharing such a raw account of his or her survey of the human experience. I'm thankful and strangely relieved to have my questions reinforced by this author's honesty. And yet, at times I can find it ultimately unsatisfying and in need of dialogue, a word from God's viewpoint. That's what I have tried to capture in this book. I find this imaginative exercise a useful and complementary example of what happens when we listen to the human author of scripture and then take time to listen to God's active voice. The result is that God, to our relief, often mirrors back to us both Divine understanding toward us and a much needed and surprising, widening perspective.

Wisdom for Old Souls is a meditation; a quiet, still chamber from which to be addressed. It is not a text to read quickly, but one to chew on in small, daily bites. Here are a few suggestions to help you engage in your own three-way dialogue with the Eternal One.

- ✦ Before reading the first entry take time to read through the entire book of Ecclesiastes. Consider using a less familiar translation. My favorite is The Voice.
- ✦ Take a moment to settle in and open your heart to what God might want to say to you. Ask God to draw your attention to what is on God's heart for you right now.
- ✦ Consider reading the colloquy from *Wisdom for Old Souls* out loud. There is something about hearing our own voice that helps us listen with "the ears of the heart."
- ✦ After reading the colloquy a few times, respond to the questions following it.
- ✦ Now shift your awareness to the presence of God and begin to write your own colloquy. Listen and write down your impression of whatever God is saying to you in response.
- ✦ As you turn toward your day, carry with you the simple word or phrase God has drawn your attention to and notice when it offers some perspective you need.

DAY ONE

These are the words of the Quester.
Ecclesiastes 1:1 (The Message)

A Colloquy

Some people think of Me as the All-Wise-One; as if I am wisdom personified. I know they mean well, but don't reduce me to an image of the impersonal and aloof professor or an ancient sage-like guru. Think of Me as a fertile, rich field. I am like a garden, one you never planted, yet are freely, lovingly invited to enter. What's holding you back?

I'm encouraging you, My old friend. Gather up and enjoy the richest of foods you find. Come in. Come in and listen. Come in and harvest as much of Me as you can carry. Then you will have true wisdom simply because you have Me. Search your heart— isn't that what you really want? It's what I want for you!

Your Turn to Respond

✦ What word or phrase are you drawn to today and why?

✦ How does the reading relate to you and your life today?

✦ What would you like to say to God?

✦ What does God want to say to you? Listen.

DAY TWO

Life is fleeting, like a passing mist.
It is like trying to catch hold of a breath;
All vanishes like a vapor; everything is a great vanity.
Ecclesiastes 1:2 (The Voice)

A Colloquy

My old friend, I want you to know that I have designed life, all life, including yours, to be fleeting, an evaporating mist. I have made it so, as if to hold on to life would be like trying to hold your breath—impossible beyond a few struggling, unnatural minutes. I have made life vanish like a vapor. It feels like a vain enterprise, but it is not. It is forever temporary, provisional, transitional, and impermanent. Yet that does not mean it is not precious. It is highly precious in its impermanence. Learn to treasure each passing minute, while at the same time not clinging to it, trusting that there is always something more, something next.

Your Turn to Respond

✤ What word or phrase are you drawn to today and why?

✤ How does the reading relate to you and your life today?

✤ What would you like to say to God?

✤ What does God want to say to you? Listen.

DAY THREE

What good does it do anyone to work so hard again and again,
sunup to sundown? All this labor to gain but a little?
Ecclesiastes 1:3 (The Voice)

A Colloquy

*No matter how hard you work, My old friend, you cannot undo this reality that I
have programmed into everything. When you strive and strain, you turn each day
into a contest of wills. You deplete all your energy in what in the end will be shown
to be mere shadow boxing. What good can ultimately come from this bare-knuckled
approach to life? In the end, such labor will always be a fool's errand. Receive your life
as a breath. Now, release it. Don't work so hard to hold on to your life. Simply be like
My breath; go out and then return to Me. Is that so hard to understand?*

Your Turn to Respond

♦ What word or phrase are you drawn to today and why?

♦ How does the reading relate to you and your life today?

♦ What would you like to say to God?

♦ What does God want to say to you? Listen.

DAY FOUR

One generation comes, another goes;
but the earth continues to remain.
Ecclesiastes 1:4 (The Voice)

A Colloquy

You've seen how one entire generation comes into being, rich with the virtues necessary for its times, but also blinded by undetected vices rooted in exaggerated anxieties and self-aggrandized estimations. At the same time, the previous generation disappears, gone without a trace.

Over and over again this phenomenon plays out, but this Eden-like-earth, your earthly home remains; everlasting in its own way just as I am eternal in Mine. I have made it so.

This dramatic change of epochs is as necessary as the change of seasons, My old friend. You need not despair to see your parent's generation disappear, even as you gradually become aware that yours, too, will soon be lost—just as your children and their children will someday vanish. I have made it so. But while you can, find ways to remember those who have come before. I remember them!

Your Turn to Respond

✦ What word or phrase are you drawn to today and why?

✦ How does the reading relate to you and your life today?

✦ What would you like to say to God?

✦ What does God want to say to you? Listen.

DAY FIVE

The sun rises and the sun sets,
laboring to come up quickly to its place again *and again.*
The wind in its travels blows toward the south,
then swings back around to the north.
Back and forth, returning in its circuit again *and again.*
All rivers flow to the sea, but the sea is never full.
To the place where the rivers flow,
there the water returns to flow once again.
Ecclesiastes 1:5-7 (The Voice)

A Colloquy

I have put the sun in motion to rise, again and again and again, only to slip past the horizon just as many times. No matter how many times it sets, the next morning this glowing sphere that fuels all of life diligently returns to its station and performs its necessary work.

I have also made the living winds, always moving, forever restless, rushing southward only to return, heading once again northward. Over and over and over, the vital air surrounding this planet stirs in one direction, only to change course. It's one constant, endless coming and going.

And don't forget, My old friend, I have also made the pulsing waters, traveling as on pilgrimage through gorges, rivulets, streams, and rivers, always toward the sea's elastic expanse. Yet this liquid body of waves and stillness, of ebbing and flowing somehow is never filled; it never seems satisfied. For I have made it so. These waters return to the high places, to tiny beginnings where they will innocently trickle down toward the widening shore's welcome.

How your life mirrors these movements of earth and sky, weather and water, sunrise and sunset! Look around you and listen, watch and glean My wisdom from wherever you can.

Your Turn to Respond

✤ What word or phrase are you drawn to today and why?

✤ How does the reading relate to you and your life today?

✤ What would you like to say to God?

✤ What does God want to say to you? Listen.

DAY SIX

Words, words, words! So many words!
They are wearisome things;
and yet people cannot refrain from speaking.
Ecclesiastes 1:8a (The Voice)

A Colloquy

Have you noticed how ceaseless, how anxious, how pointless so many words are? How I wish I could relieve you, My old friend, from the burden of all this endless chatter. And yet, I have made you so—a worded being—your words carving out channels of blessing as well as cursing. Your words and My words, commingling, colliding, complementing, contrasting. Can you learn to accept this? There seems to be no rest in sight from all these words. You and I just can't help but communicate.

So go ahead, don't be timid, don't withhold yourself. Initiate rich conversations with Me, as well as friends and strangers alike.

Your Turn to Respond

✦ What word or phrase are you drawn to today and why?

✦ How does the reading relate to you and your life today?

✦ What would you like to say to God?

✦ What does God want to say to you? Listen.

DAY SEVEN

No matter how much we see, we are never satisfied.
No matter how much we hear, we are not content.
Ecclesiastes 1:8b (New Living Translation)

A Colloquy

I have made your two eyes and the gift of seeing. The wonder of beholding the mundane and the marvelous comes from Me. And I have made you in such a way that your eyes will never be completely satisfied. In fact, I have made you so that your vision's restless appetite wants to take in more and more.

Along with your eyes, I have placed two ears on your head. I have given you the gift to hear creation sing, the capacity to hear Me sing My love songs, as well as the depth to be moved by the lament of My children's sorrows. With your head cocked, turning toward each direction, you tune into all that is familiar, perk up to the curious sound of something new.

Your desire to see the unseen and to hear the unheard is like a bucket without a bottom. I have made you in such a way, My old friend, that the world continually pours through all your senses and yet it never fills you to a point of complete fullness. But now, I'm asking you to really look. Really listen. And don't move on too quickly from what your senses are being drawn to notice.

Your Turn to Respond

✤ What word or phrase are you drawn to today and why?

✤ How does the reading relate to you and your life today?

✤ What would you like to say to God?

✤ What does God want to say to you? Listen.

DAY EIGHT

History merely repeats itself.
It has all been done before.
Nothing under the sun is truly new.
Ecclesiastes 1:9 (New Living Translation)

A Colloquy

What has been, what has happened, it is done. The present is always rapidly absorbed by the past and becomes something finished. But just because it is now a memory does not mean it can never be repeated. Novelty is not the only or greatest pleasure in life, My old friend. There is just as much pleasure found in a musical composition's refrain as there is in the introduction of a new motif. Learn to embrace both the repetitive sounds and the emergent surprises. What ambient sounds are so familiar to you right now that they pass by unnoticed, unrecognized for their enduring goodness?

Your Turn to Respond

✤ What word or phrase are you drawn to today and why?

✤ How does the reading relate to you and your life today?

✤ What would you like to say to God?

✤ What does God want to say to you? Listen.

DAY NINE

One person may say of some idea,
"Pay attention to this; it's original!"
But that same idea has already been expressed;
it's been with us through the ages.

Ecclesiastes 1:10 (The Voice)

A Colloquy

So, don't despair, My old friend, when the experience of your one, unique life suddenly seems quite unexceptional. All of your inspirations, all of your ways of grasping life's meaning are common to all My children. All people grapple with fears and dreams, each one unknowingly drawing upon the grace I have poured out from the beginning on the entire earth. In fact this common grace and your common experience of it expresses a beautiful continuity. It grounds you in humility and delivers you from pride's burden of trying to be something you're not. Give up all your attempts to be more special. You are thoroughly special already.

Your Turn to Respond

❋ What word or phrase are you drawn to today and why?

❋ How does the reading relate to you and your life today?

❋ What would you like to say to God?

❋ What does God want to say to you? Listen.

DAY TEN

We don't remember what happened in the past,
and in future generations, no one will remember what we are doing now.
Ecclesiastes 1:11 (New Living Translation)

A Colloquy

Do not despair, My old friend, that I made you largely incapable of remembering those who preceded you; what they may have accomplished or what they left unfinished. This includes even your direct and immediate ancestors. It's a strange mercy, but in the same way, you, too, will quickly be forgotten. Whether you want to or not, you will make room—mental as well as physical—for all who are yet to come.

If your memory did not fade so swiftly, your attention would always be filtered, and thoughts continuously weighed down by all that has come before you. I want each generation to experience their lives utterly free, as an unscripted possibility, not blindly living out of the programming of something that has happened before. Don't let the shadows of those who have come before you confine you to their dreams and commitments. Live your life, not theirs.

Your Turn to Respond

❖ What word or phrase are you drawn to today and why?

❖ How does the reading relate to you and your life today?

❖ What would you like to say to God?

❖ What does God want to say to you? Listen.

DAY ELEVEN

I decided to seek out and study the wisdom *of the ages,*
of all that had been done under the heavens.
I soon discovered the harsh realities
of the work God has given us that keeps us so busy.
Ecclesiastes 1:13 (The Voice)

A Colloquy

My old friend, you have an explorer's spirit akin to Mine. I, too, possess a deep and perpetual curiosity, a deep well of endless inquisitiveness. Keep seeking wisdom, and you will find it. Everything that is or has been is like an open book for those wanting to delve into the mysteries.

But know this: you will also uncover many hard truths, aspects of our shared reality that are confusing and painful. Your life's work will often feel like more than you can bear. Remember, even when it does, that you will learn to bear it. In fact, you must bear it, even as I, too, bear it all. Tell me, is there something in your present situation or current vocation that feels more like a cross than a crown?

Your Turn to Respond

+ What word or phrase are you drawn to today and why?

+ How does the reading relate to you and your life today?

+ What would you like to say to God?

+ What does God want to say to you? Listen.

DAY TWELVE

I have witnessed all that is done under the sun, and indeed,
all is fleeting, like trying to embrace the wind.
Ecclesiastes 1:14 (The Voice)

A Colloquy

*If you can fathom it, My old friend, I have fully experienced each and every moment
of time, each person's life in minute detail since the beginning of this planet's long and
evolving history. At the time, to each man and woman, the steps they took, the choices
they made, were utterly real, meaningful, important.*

*But now, in retrospect, can you see how I have made time's flow fleeting? I have made
it so that trying to hold on to one's life is as futile as attempting to hug a cloud. Have
you ever stopped to consider your perspective, your beliefs and assumptions about
time? It's hard, I know, since you swim in time as a fish swims downstream in the
irresistible flow of a river? But isn't it about time to consider time?*

Your Turn to Respond

◆ What word or phrase are you drawn to today and why?

◆ How does the reading relate to you and your life today?

◆ What would you like to say to God?

◆ What does God want to say to you? Listen.

DAY THIRTEEN

There is an old saying:
Something crooked cannot be made straight,
and something missing cannot be counted.
Ecclesiastes 1:15 (The Voice)

A Colloquy

One of earth's long forgotten sages said somewhere:

> *All that is twisted is twisted and cannot be untwisted.*
> *So, don't try to make up for what is missing.*
> *For what is missing is missing.*
> *It can never be recovered by the fantasy of a time machine.*

It's up to you, My old friend, to only change what can be changed and to realistically mend whatever can still be mended. You'll find this more than enough challenge for your hands and your heart. Where are you spending precious energy to undo what can't be undone; or trying to do what is not yours to do?

Your Turn to Respond

❦ What word or phrase are you drawn to today and why?

❦ How does the reading relate to you and your life today?

❦ What would you like to say to God?

❦ What does God want to say to you? Listen.

DAY FOURTEEN

I mused over it all and thought to myself, "I have done great things,
and I have gained more wisdom than anyone who reigned over Jerusalem
before me. I have contemplated great wisdom and knowledge."
I decided to study wisdom and instead acquainted myself with madness
and folly. It, too, seemed like trying to pursue the wind,
for as my wisdom increased, so did my vexation.
As my knowledge grew, so did my pain.
Ecclesiastes 1:16-18 (The Voice)

A Colloquy

Some of your kind, My old friend, in their arrogance and self-aggrandizement will believe they have more insight and wisdom than all those around them. Some may unconsciously devote themselves to the swinging pendulum of extremes, first pursuing every new and shimmering shard of wisdom, only to be later consumed by all kinds of irrational, uncontrolled compulsions. Have you seen this? Or maybe this is still your hopelessly disenchanting experience.

You can follow that trail, My old friend, but know for certain that at some point, if you have not lost touch with reality, you will find yourself in a cyclone's eye of frustration. You will end up just like a dog chasing its tail, round and round, mesmerized by the pursuit of each new shiny object, only to be shocked at the self-inflicted pain of your own jaws clamping down on the meaningless wagging of your own rear end. It's better to be neither too wise and measured in your own eyes, nor too compulsive and out of control in the eyes of others.

Your Turn to Respond

✦ What word or phrase are you drawn to today and why?

✦ How does the reading relate to you and your life today?

✦ What would you like to say to God?

✦ What does God want to say to you? Listen.

DAY FIFTEEN

I said to myself, "Come on, let's try pleasure.
Let's look for the 'good things' in life."
But I found that this, too, was meaningless.
So I said, "Laughter is silly. What good does it do to seek pleasure?"
Ecclesiastes 2:1-2 (New Living Translation)

A Colloquy

You see, My old friend, contrary to what many imagine, I am the One who created pleasure along with all which brings you pleasure. However there are some, who in their restless and twisted circling to find something of comfort, only wind up in an endless chase for what merely feels good. They forget that authentic pleasure is always the blessed fruit of the life I am giving them, not the root. This pleasure seeking, in and of itself, will always end in tasteless emptiness.

But don't think Me a prude. And don't be shocked. I love a good joke more than you can imagine. Yet always chasing after the next laugh is also ultimately hollow—as shallow as living life as a constant pursuit of serial pleasures. Can you imagine how empty it is to seek a constant buzz all day, every day? Wine is for celebration, but your life is far richer than visiting one party after another.

I'd like you to consider for a moment where some of your pleasure seeking might be taking you. But I'd also like you to hear My invitation to have more fun and learn to play more. Does that sound contradictory?

Your Turn to Respond

✦ What word or phrase are you drawn to today and why?

✦ How does the reading relate to you and your life today?

✦ What would you like to say to God?

✦ What does God want to say to you? Listen.

DAY SIXTEEN

After much thought, I decided to cheer myself with wine.
And while still seeking wisdom, I clutched at foolishness.
In this way, I tried to experience the only happiness most people find
during their brief life in this world.

Ecclesiastes 2:3 (New Living Translation)

A Colloquy

My old friend, as you seek to find a meaningful pathway through what could quickly become an endless maze of compulsive escapes, keep a wise head about it all. Wisdom can bring you back to love's center. Wisdom can help you live each day as if it is your last. Wisdom will remind you that your last day, along with all you cherish, will arrive all too soon. How does it make you feel to consider the end, your end? That someday you will say goodbye to everyone and everything you love?

Your Turn to Respond

✦ What word or phrase are you drawn to today and why?

✦ How does the reading relate to you and your life today?

✦ What would you like to say to God?

✦ What does God want to say to you? Listen.

DAY SEVENTEEN

Throughout this experiment, I let myself have anything my eyes desired,
and I did not withhold from my mind any pleasure.
Ecclesiastes 2:10a (The Voice)

A Colloquy

*Some of you, because of your privileged position in life, will go all out to achieve,
to acquire, to outdo others. Your houses, your grounds will be carefully designed to
impress and inspire. These monuments to self will be filled with beautiful form and
impressive function, but you will still find, after surveying all that you have done, that
your gnawing, hungry heart and weary eyes lack fulfillment.*

*And yet, My old friend, knowing all this, you seem to not be able to restrain yourself.
The ever-present drive to measure your life by your accumulations has become as
addictive as the most powerful drug on the planet. In these impressive, yet blind
pursuits, you will use and abuse everyone around you to achieve what others can only
dream of. Unsatisfied with all that you amass, you may even give into the temptation
of shallow, relational experiences fueled by lustful pleasures and illusions.*

*Over-achieving. Over-indulging. In the end what's gained? What's been the cost?
Having tasted all you are driven to experience, you will all too soon exit this life in
the same manner as everyone else. It's unavoidable. Death and dying are the shared
endpoint common to all, whether pampered or exhausted.*

Your Turn to Respond

✦ What word or phrase are you drawn to today and why?

✦ How does the reading relate to you and your life today?

✦ What would you like to say to God?

✦ What does God want to say to you? Listen.

DAY EIGHTEEN

What was the conclusion?
My mind found joy in all the work I did—
my work was its own reward!
As I continued musing over all I had accomplished
and the hard work it took,
I concluded that all this, too, was fleeting,
like trying to embrace the wind.
Is there any real gain by all our hard work under the sun?
Ecclesiastes 2:10b-11 (The Voice)

A Colloquy

I have designed life, My old friend, so that it is in your embracing the actual methods you employ, in being present to the moments of challenging work, and in your intelligent craftsmanship that you will experience true joy. Never forget this, or you will set yourself up for endless frustration. The final results of all your work are ever fleeting, like trying to prevent an ice cube from melting in the desert sun. It is your experience and then your body and mind's memory of being joyfully present to those experiences that will remain. All else will be shown as hopelessly transitory sooner or later. Learn to inhabit the process of all you do. That's what you will remember. That's what you will carry with you. Why deny yourself the joy that comes from being fully present as you work, no matter how mundane or challenging?

Your Turn to Respond

✤ What word or phrase are you drawn to today and why?

✤ How does the reading relate to you and your life today?

✤ What would you like to say to God?

✤ What does God want to say to you? Listen.

DAY NINETEEN

I turned my attention to the ways of wisdom and folly and madness.
I asked, "What is left for those who come after the king to do?
They can only repeat what he has already done."
I realized that wisdom is better than folly, just as light is better than darkness.
As the old saying goes:
The wise have eyes in their heads, but fools stumble in the darkness.
Yet I knew deep down that the same fate comes to both of them.
Ecclesiastes 2:12-14 (The Voice)

A Colloquy

So much of life, of your life, My old friend, remains hidden to you. In your late-night ponderings to make sense of it, you will often vacillate between playing the wise man or woman, and then playing the fool. You may at times even feel yourself plunging into existential madness, losing your grip on reality as you have previously understood it. You will at times feel despairing boredom. Nothing you do seems truly original. You seem destined to only repeat what every human has done who has come before you.

Yet if you do not let this despair carry you away, you will see that My wisdom is your true home. You will know for yourself where the pursuit of folly will take you; down a blind alley from which you will suffer, then seek to exit.

After having seen so many ways and tried so many things, are you at last resolved to turn your attention toward Me for the perspective you say you need? Never forget, the door to My wisdom always swings open for you and welcomes you to come further in.

Your Turn to Respond

✦ What word or phrase are you drawn to today and why?

✦ How does the reading relate to you and your life today?

✦ What would you like to say to God?

✦ What does God want to say to you? Listen.

DAY TWENTY

When I realized that my fate's the same as the fool's, I had to ask myself,
"So why bother being wise?" It's all smoke, nothing but smoke.
The smart and the stupid both disappear out of sight.
In a day or two they're both forgotten.
Yes, both the smart and the stupid die, and that's it.
I hate life. As far as I can see, what happens on earth is a bad business.
It's smoke—and spitting into the wind.
Ecclesiastes 215-:17 (The Message)

A Colloquy

It's an irrefutable fact, My old friend, for I have made it so: whether you pursue patterns of wisdom or illusions of folly, each one comes to the same end. It will seem to you that life has hardly started before it is over. Knowing this can fill you with a deep melancholy as you realize how quickly all traces of that which was will disappear. Your entire life, like the pulling of your finger out of the ocean's churning water, will scarcely leave an impression beyond a few fading ripples.

Try not to despair. I know how hard, even unbearable, this knowledge can seem at times. But your life has immense value. Even though it is ephemeral in its beauty and goodness, it is incredibly treasured by Me—all of it—especially your tears, your doubts, and your questions. Will you let Me reassure you? Even when it seems without any point or lasting meaning, it's all worthwhile, it all matters deeply to Me because you matter to Me!

Your Turn to Respond

✦ What word or phrase are you drawn to today and why?

✦ How does the reading relate to you and your life today?

✦ What would you like to say to God?

✦ What does God want to say to you? Listen.

DAY TWENTY-ONE

I came to hate all my hard work here on earth,
for I must leave to others everything I have earned.
And who can tell whether my successors will be wise or foolish?
Yet they will control everything I have gained by my skill and hard work
under the sun. How meaningless! So I gave up in despair,
questioning the value of all my hard work in this world.
Some people work wisely with knowledge and skill,
then must leave the fruit of their efforts to someone who hasn't worked for it.
This, too, is meaningless, a great tragedy.
So what do people get in this life for all their hard work and anxiety?
Their days of labor are filled with pain and grief; even at night their minds
cannot rest. It is all meaningless.
Ecclesiastes 2:18-23 (New Living Translation)

A Colloquy

My old friend, you may not understand this now, but I am showing you how My grace operates in this realm of reality. For the wise, faithful, diligent, hard-working man or woman, grace can easily be obscured by an attempt to be rewarded for "doing things right." It shocks you even now to learn that My blessings flow directly to all and through all, the wise and the foolish alike. It will surprise you to know firsthand that in the end, neither your wisdom nor work ethic will add anything to your place with Me. And in the same way, no one's fickleness or foolishness will diminish who they are to Me. Because of this, I have designed life in such a way to continually recirculate temporal blessings, completely disregarding the notion of merits. This is the logic of grace; a logic so difficult for the wise and the moral to comprehend.

Seek with all your heart to gain My perspective. Don't work harder than your life circumstances deem necessary. Accept that there will be hard days, hard things to do, but don't become a martyr and make them harder than they need to be. Learn to rest. Rest in grace, so you don't let the real or imagined stresses invade your dreams and rob you of a good night's sleep.

Your Turn to Respond

❖ What word or phrase are you drawn to today and why?

❖ How does the reading relate to you and your life today?

❖ What would you like to say to God?

❖ What does God want to say to you? Listen.

DAY TWENTY-TWO

There is nothing better than for people to eat and drink
and to see the good in their hard work.
These beautiful gifts, I realized, too, come from God's hand.
For who can eat and drink and enjoy the good things if not me?
To those who seek to please God,
He gives wisdom and knowledge and joyfulness;
but to those who are wicked, God keeps them busy harvesting and storing up
for those in whom He delights.
But even this is fleeting; it's like trying to embrace the wind.
Ecclesiastes 2:24-26 (The Voice)

A Colloquy

Take My advice, old friend. After all, this was My idea to begin with! Eat—taste your food, let its flavors excite your taste buds. And drink—share a glass of fine wine with friends and strangers alike. Then look deeply into the heart of your true vocation. Tell Me—what do you see? When you perceive the essence of your lifework, don't you see the simple goodness of it? Rejoice! Not just in the results of your skills and labor, but delight in the entire process, even the difficult and distasteful.

For if you don't, it will all feel like busy work—as if I'm a stingy, overbearing boss who just wants to get rich off any poor devil's back who's too stupid to care. I delight in each one of you. I delight in it all. Yet there are many who see only wickedness when they consider life, even when they consider Me—and especially when they consider themselves. Can't you see how damning this point of view is; how nothing meaningful can ever come of it? How does your approach to life and your lifework need to be reframed?

Your Turn to Respond

✤ What word or phrase are you drawn to today and why?

✤ How does the reading relate to you and your life today?

✤ What would you like to say to God?

✤ What does God want to say to you? Listen.

DAY TWENTY-THREE

For everything there is a season
and a time for every matter under heaven.
Ecclesiastes 3:1 (New Revised Standard Version)

A Colloquy

I want you to know, My old friend, that I have made time, too. This mysterious yet ubiquitous reality that embraces everything. You see, time, as I have designed it, is not simply another thing, but rather an empty space, an ever expanding and contracting receptacle. In time all things are possible. Your life is always flowing within the givens of Chronos and Kairos, back and forth between the probable and the improbable, the possible and the impossible, the necessary and the unnecessary.

And so a day of your life can yawn before you in sleepy contentment; it can gape like an open wound; or sometimes growl like an empty stomach. Your feelings about the future and about time itself say much about you. How do you feel as you consider your future and the time yet ahead?

Your Turn to Respond

✦ What word or phrase are you drawn to today and why?

✦ How does the reading relate to you and your life today?

✦ What would you like to say to God?

✦ What does God want to say to you? Listen.

DAY TWENTY-FOUR

A time to be born, a time to die;
a time to plant, a time to collect the harvest.
Ecclesiastes 3:2 (The Voice)

A Colloquy

The day of your birth, My old friend, is a day of joy to Me, as will be the moment of your death. These seminal minutes surrounding your beginning and ending will frame every experience you have during your earthly lifetime. Can you see this now? Can you see Me now, with you up to the very end?

Within this life you have many seasons of preparing the soil, planting seeds, and watering small green shoots. These days will then blossom into fruitful pursuits, into times of harvest. Find new energy to gather whatever the processes of growth have produced at your feet and under your care.

Your Turn to Respond

✤ What word or phrase are you drawn to today and why?

✤ How does the reading relate to you and your life today?

✤ What would you like to say to God?

✤ What does God want to say to you? Listen.

DAY TWENTY-FIVE

A time to kill and a time to heal;
a time to break down and a time to build up.
Ecclesiastes 3:3 (New Revised Standard Version)

A Colloquy

It is a hard reality to accept, My old friend, but there will be times when something, or even someone, will need to die so that you may continue to live. This cosmic fact will be balanced with My miraculous law of healing; an energy I have placed within the very cells of your body, a gift that can be activated through your healer's mind and hands.

Because of the unyielding nature of change, there will be times when humanity's amazing creations as well as your diabolical systems and structures will need to be destroyed. There is a grace in this, too. I have made it so. But then, if you are patient, out of the rubble, new materials, new tools and toys, new arrangements will be designed and brought into existence. May they all emerge to bless more than they harm. We shall see.

Your Turn to Respond

❖ What word or phrase are you drawn to today and why?

❖ How does the reading relate to you and your life today?

❖ What would you like to say to God?

❖ What does God want to say to you? Listen.

DAY TWENTY-SIX

A time to cry, a time to laugh;
a time to mourn, a time to dance.
Ecclesiastes 3:4 (The Voice)

A Colloquy

My old friend, does it surprise you that I truly mourn more than all others? Or laugh with more gusto than all creation combined? Because I am so moved, all your tears flow into mine, and your chuckles and giggles combine with My amusement and reverberate our shared joy.

When you mourn, I mourn. Can you feel the depth of My sadness surrounding and embracing our shared losses? Does it surprise you that losses in life pierce My heart, just as your losses pierce yours?

But tears are for a season, then miraculously the clouds part, the clear blue sky reappears, and the warmth of the bright, radiant sun moves us both to kick the dust off our shoes; to dance, and spin, and smile, and almost forget what had made us so sad. Almost.

Can you begin to give Me access to your true feelings? Not in order that I might eliminate them, but to share with one another how life is impacting us. You see, I also long to be pursued by you, to be known by you, and for you to treasure My emotional connections and movements.

Your Turn to Respond

✦ What word or phrase are you drawn to today and why?

✦ How does the reading relate to you and your life today?

✦ What would you like to say to God?

✦ What does God want to say to you? Listen.

DAY TWENTY-SEVEN

A time to scatter stones and a time to gather them.
Ecclesiastes 3:5a (New International Version)

A Colloquy

There are times for walking along the seashore to pick up flat, smooth stones to cram into every pocket you have. Collecting is fun. It can be purposeful too. But a time comes, My old friend, when what you've gathered will weigh you down and rip your bulging pockets if you continue to hoard everything you can possibly pick up. Then you know it's time to empty every one; from your shirt, your jacket, your pants—and then take the pile of stones you've stacked on the shore and skip them on still waters. Maybe one bounce, sometimes two and once in a while they may even skitter a dozen times. To skip a stone, you must first pick it up. But if it stays in your pocket, what's the fun in that?

You've collected many of My blessings along the way. Some are real treasures, aren't they? It's brought Me pleasure to see how you've enjoyed them. But now, don't you think it's about time to scatter some of them about? Where do you want to start?

Your Turn to Respond

❖ What word or phrase are you drawn to today and why?

❖ How does the reading relate to you and your life today?

❖ What would you like to say to God?

❖ What does God want to say to you? Listen.

DAY TWENTY-EIGHT

A time for a warm embrace, a time for keeping your distance.
Ecclesiastes 3:5b (The Voice)

A Colloquy

My old friend, I've given you and your people two arms. There's so much you can do with them. But above all else, I've designed your arms to embrace all you meet. And then, when the time is right, to be embraced in return.

Yet I know it's hard for you to imagine not opening your arms to everyone. In an innocent world, a world for which you have been designed, you could. But you don't live in absolute paradise now, do you? So accept this, too. There will be times when it's best for you and for others to pull away and refrain from such an embrace.

Establishing and honoring one another's boundaries is also an expression of love. And sometimes, your refusal to embrace others too quickly, especially when they've been hurtful to you or others or even themselves will cause them to take stock. Triggering a disconnection with someone like that is an opportunity to disrupt an unloving way of relating. Hopefully then, in time, you can both return and offer one another a shared embrace.

Your Turn to Respond

✤ What word or phrase are you drawn to today and why?

✤ How does the reading relate to you and your life today?

✤ What would you like to say to God?

✤ What does God want to say to you? Listen.

DAY TWENTY-NINE

A time to search, a time to give up as lost.
Ecclesiastes 3:6a (The Voice)

A Colloquy

My old friend, there will be many confusing times ahead. The path will not always be entirely clear to you, yet you will be confronted with the need to make a hard decision. For instance, there will be relationships, people, things, and patterns of living that may up to this point have been true blessings, but now they have become lost on you. You will find yourself earnestly seeking and trying to recover what's missing. It may feel like an ache or, even worse, an amputation. At some point, in spite of everything, if you still can't find what's been lost, you will realize (even with great sadness) that it is time to call off the search and move on.

Your Turn to Respond

+ What word or phrase are you drawn to today and why?

+ How does the reading relate to you and your life today?

+ What would you like to say to God?

+ What does God want to say to you? Listen.

DAY THIRTY

A time to keep and a time to throw away
Ecclesiastes 3:6b (New Living Translation)

A Colloquy

My old friend, there will be things you have attentively cared for (maybe for years or decades); prized possessions, revered institutions, cherished ideas, or beliefs and opinions. Then one day, as you hold them before your heart and mind in a new light, you will conclude that it is time to disentangle from your attachment. It may feel like you're throwing overboard some antiquated, yet valuable cargo from this lifeboat of yours. But can't you see that there will be storms ahead to weather, crossings and voyages to navigate, that will necessitate lightening your load? Otherwise you will sink from all that extra weight or simply drag bottom, impossibly overburdened, unable to leave the harbor.

What's weighing you down? I see it, do you? Don't worry, I won't pry it from your hands—that's for you to do. But for your sake I hope you will choose to lighten your load so that you will be ready for whatever life brings next.

Your Turn to Respond

✤ What word or phrase are you drawn to today and why?

✤ How does the reading relate to you and your life today?

✤ What would you like to say to God?

✤ What does God want to say to you? Listen.

DAY THIRTY-ONE

A time to tear apart, a time to bind together.
Ecclesiastes 3:7a (The Voice)

A Colloquy

Creative acts are always messy. In the process of doing what is in your heart, My old friend, there will be times of destroying, times of tearing apart. It will often seem like you're even making things worse. The risk of undoing something is a necessary step in the art of creative love and creative work. But eventually, there comes the moment to put it back together, to reassemble materials and even relationships in new ways. Isn't this what a surgeon does? Isn't this what a carpenter does? Cutting, stitching, nailing, healing, creating. Jump into My creative process with Me! What's holding you back? Don't overthink it, just take the first step. I'll be there with you through the whole process.

Your Turn to Respond

✦ What word or phrase are you drawn to today and why?

✦ How does the reading relate to you and your life today?

✦ What would you like to say to God?

✦ What does God want to say to you? Listen.

DAY THIRTY-TWO

A time to be quiet, a time to speak up.
Ecclesiastes 3:7b (The Voice)

A Colloquy

Have you noticed how much confusion there is in both your silence and your words? Often you find that when it would be wise to keep your mouth shut, you lack restraint, and say things that hurt, or make things worse, or simply cloud an already complicated state of affairs. Then there are other times when a kind word, or even a bold word is called for. And what do you do? You retract your head like a timid little turtle and think you are safe in your shell of silence.

I want you, My old friend, to speak up and speak out. And I want both your words and your tone to be birthed from the quiet depths of My love. My love will show you when to break your silence as well as when to return to it. Listen to your heart. You know who needs to hear from you today. And you also know who needs your listening ear.

Your Turn to Respond

✦ What word or phrase are you drawn to today and why?

✦ How does the reading relate to you and your life today?

✦ What would you like to say to God?

✦ What does God want to say to you? Listen.

DAY THIRTY-THREE

A time to love and a time to hate
Ecclesiastes 3:8a (New International Version)

A Colloquy

You will discover, My old friend, that there is an oppositional dynamic necessary in each child's makeup. The word "no" is the mark of a "self" having arrived on the scene. Consider it a cosmic principle, like gravity.

But where you begin is not where you are to end up. This simplistic, two-dimensional, no/yes dualism of childhood must be transcended if you are to become My adult son or daughter. You will find love and hate to be one of these troubling dualisms. You must above all else seek to integrate both, otherwise you will become another vain caricature of My glory.

If you have only love, never being disgusted or repulsed by anything, you will become a walking marshmallow; soft and sweet, but having no substance, no grit. But, if your identity is absorbed by all that you despise, if your orientation is one of constant judgment and condemnation, you will find yourself hopelessly imprisoned whether you stand on the right or the left.

I long for you to love openly, freely, and wildly all whom you meet—just like Me. Don't hold back. But as you love fiercely, you will at times be called upon to oppose destructive evil, hurtful people, and tyrannical structures. This vital energy, experienced as hatred, will serve love. How is it for you to integrate this powerful dynamic—to love well and to exercise opposition in the service of love? I know it's not easy.

Your Turn to Respond

+ What word or phrase are you drawn to today and why?

+ How does the reading relate to you and your life today?

+ What would you like to say to God?

+ What does God want to say to you? Listen.

DAY THIRTY-FOUR

A right time to wage war and another to make peace.
Ecclesiastes 3:8b (The Message)

A Colloquy

A just war, if you want to call it that, is still exactly that: war. Whether you fight for those who are vulnerable, war against evil; don't shrink back from culture's brokenness that wounds and abuses on a massive, global scale, it's still war. But in your righteous frenzy and fury, realize this: war and all warring are only for a season. Your fighting, My old friend, is to be actively and permanently coupled with peace-making. Never let peace disappear from your field of vision. Otherwise, at some point, a peaceful warrior will be needed to come and wage war against your growing appetite to do violence.

You can get stuck in enemy mode, you know. Begin to notice this in your body, as well as the exaggerated feelings of fear, mistrust, and aggressiveness. My peace is both subjective and objective. But if you can't feel My peace, it's unlikely that you will disarm yourself and begin to love your enemy.

Your Turn to Respond

✤ What word or phrase are you drawn to today and why?

✤ How does the reading relate to you and your life today?

✤ What would you like to say to God?

✤ What does God want to say to you? Listen.

DAY THIRTY-FIVE

What do people really get for all their hard work?
I have seen the burden God has placed on us all.
Yet God has made everything beautiful for its own time.
Ecclesiastes 3:9-11a (New Living Translation)

A Colloquy

I see your anxious striving, My old friend, your restless ego's quest to prove and protect yourself. Let Me remind you to simply give yourself to the good work that presents itself. The real reward is in the work itself, not the power or allure of endless acquisition. Your needs, as well as the subtle nudges from My Creative Spirit within you, will occupy you quite sufficiently.

We are co-laborers. We are partners. The drive to prove yourself was never from Me. That quest was settled even before you were born. When you and I are working side by side, hand in hand, we can creatively produce what we set out to do, no matter how small or challenging, how trivial or world altering. It's an incredible gift to notice how good and beautiful this life can be.

I know that this can sound too good to be true and often it's not where you find yourself. So tell Me, what about your vocation is the cause of this stress in you? Is it the work itself, or is it something deeper, something more essential and elusive to your well-being? Can you identify and name what seems to be provoking your anxious thoughts and actions around your work?

Your Turn to Respond

❖ What word or phrase are you drawn to today and why?

❖ How does the reading relate to you and your life today?

❖ What would you like to say to God?

❖ What does God want to say to you? Listen.

DAY THIRTY-SIX

He has planted eternity in the human heart, but even so,
people cannot see the whole scope of God's work from beginning to end.
Ecclesiastes 3:11b (New Living Translation)

A Colloquy

*Does your life sometimes confuse you, My old friend? I don't mean the circumstances
of your life or the external things, I mean your inner life. When you look inside, are
you sometimes baffled? I hope so. For I have placed the long shadow of My very
essence in the core of that which you know as yourself. You can never escape, never
run away from My mysterious presence deep within. That includes even the times
when you detach from the present moment and slip into your rumination of past
successes and failures or your speculations about what lies ahead, whether tragedies or
fantasies. Settle, instead, into the mystery with Me. For we are always, both of us, far,
far more than we appear.*

*Even if it's overwhelming at times, I want you to not shrink back or ignore the journey
of uncovering your true, authentic self, the real you. It's never self-indulgent to get a
clearer picture of who you are to Me and who I've made you to be in My world.*

Your Turn to Respond

❧ What word or phrase are you drawn to today and why?

❧ How does the reading relate to you and your life today?

❧ What would you like to say to God?

❧ What does God want to say to you? Listen.

DAY THIRTY-SEVEN

I know there is nothing better for us than to be joyful
and to do good throughout our lives;
to eat and drink and see the good in all of our
hard work is a gift from God.
Ecclesiastes 3:12-13 (The Voice)

A Colloquy

*Does it surprise you, My old friend, that your highest good, what I have made you for,
is nothing less than My joy? To experience My joy over you, as well as your joy over
Me and all I have created, is My master key to life. This universal key unlocks every
door. I want you to know that it is joy, not your morality or truth or any other old
worn key, which will unlock the truly good life for you.*

*As you enter into My open and spacious heart through this doorway, you will
experience a single and unified freedom; the freedom of your humanity, the freedom of
divinity enfleshed in your flesh. You will then eat with gratitude and gusto, drink with
delight and devotion, work with passion and even pain, grasping how all these tangible
features of your one authentic life are saturated with My goodness. Can you recognize
the truth in this yet? Can you identify the lies that play in your head that get in the
way of believing it's true?*

Your Turn to Respond

✦ What word or phrase are you drawn to today and why?

✦ How does the reading relate to you and your life today?

✦ What would you like to say to God?

✦ What does God want to say to you? Listen.

DAY THIRTY-EIGHT

I know everything God does endures for all time.
Nothing can be added to it; nothing can be taken away from it.
We humans can only stand in awe of all God has done.
What has been and what is to be—already is.
And God holds accountable all the pursuits of humanity
Ecclesiastes 3:14-15 (The Voice)

A Colloquy

I'll let you in on one of My little secrets, old friend. Everything I do, each thought I have, each emotion I feel—all of it—is eternal, just as I am eternal. What does that mean for you? Since all My thoughts, feelings, and acts toward you, toward all I've made, are expressions of eternal and creative love, nothing you do or fail to do can ever add to or subtract from the affection I have for you. When you hear lofty words about Me, or My glory, or My holiness, or My eternal nature, this is what it means to Me. To be in awe of Me means only one thing: that My creative love for you is experienced as a gushing geyser erupting from a reservoir that has no end!

In spite of any and all changes in your circumstances, you are always held by Me. I am always present to what is and not what should be or could have been. All I ask of you, all I have ever wanted from you, is for your good. Above all, I desire that—like Me—you, too, may live your days in the pursuit and expression of creative love.

Think for a moment of what that might look like in your day today. Where might you walk the path of creative love with more awareness and intention?

Your Turn to Respond

❖ What word or phrase are you drawn to today and why?

❖ How does the reading relate to you and your life today?

❖ What would you like to say to God?

❖ What does God want to say to you? Listen.

DAY THIRTY-NINE

I also noticed that under the sun there is evil in the courtroom.
Yes, even the courts of law are corrupt! I said to myself,
"In due season God will judge everyone,
both good and bad, for all their deeds."
I also thought about the human condition—
how God proves to people that they are like animals.
For people and animals share the same fate—
both breathe and both must die.
So people have no real advantage over the animals.
How meaningless! Both go to the same place—
they came from dust and they return to dust.
For who can prove that the human spirit goes up
and the spirit of animals goes down into the earth.
So I saw that there is nothing better for people
than to be happy in their work. That is our lot in life.
And no one can bring us back to see what happens after we die.
Ecclesiastes 3:16-22 (New Living Translation)

A Colloquy

I know, My old friend, that when you look at the way things are for you and your fellow humans, things seem so inverted. You would not be wrong to conclude that in the majority of cases, doing the hurtful thing, committing the wrongful act, the unjust act, is rewarded by the logic of your culture. Others before you have set up the rules as a game where the winner takes all. What this devolves into is a mutant humanity that reproduces men and women who are driven to become shark-like predators.

As you know all too well, these predators invariably climb to the top of the food chain. From that seemingly untouchable position, they appear invincible. It's shocking, even liberating to know that in the end, the despised wriggling shrew along with the majestic soaring eagle will both dissolve into the earth as all other living beings who have come before. How can you resolve the seeming absurdity of it all where neither prey nor predator, in the end, are better off in the place of their finishing?

As I have tried to tell you before, simply live each day with creative presence. This alone will bring you joy. Not your cultures' fighting and defending, continually obsessed to win against a real or imagined foe. Where's the joy in living life as a battlefield? Do you want to be remembered for your anxious aggression or your grounded generativity?

Your Turn to Respond

✦ What word or phrase are you drawn to today and why?

✦ How does the reading relate to you and your life today?

✦ What would you like to say to God?

✦ What does God want to say to you? Listen.

DAY FORTY

Then I looked again and saw all the oppression
that happens under the sun.
I saw the tears of the oppressed,
and no one offered to help and comfort them.
The oppressors exercise all the power, while the powerless
have no one to help and comfort them.
It struck me that the dead are actually better off
than the living who must go on living;
and, even better, are those who were never born in the first place.
At least they have never had to witness
all of the injustices that take place under the sun.
Ecclesiastes 4:1-3 (The Voice)

A Colloquy

The eyes I have given you can't help but scan the horizon, noticing life's goodness and its oppressiveness. I see it, too. I see you, too, My old friend. I see you when you are beaten down, alone, with no one to help. I see others as they cry out for relief, only to be met with the unbearable demands of the powerful, the inhumane standards of the privileged. I see your empty, hollow eyes, staring into the abyss, starved for a scrap of human tenderness, a kind word of comfort.

When you arrive at the depths of desolation in your life's journey, it can feel like death is the better option, maybe even your only option. You may at times regret that you ever came into being. At least then, you reason, you would not have been traumatized by the world's pervading, brutal injustices. I understand how you long to unsee many of the things your eyes have seen?

What do you want Me to say? You have seen and experienced too much to be soothed by the pacifier of pretty words. All I can offer you is this: you are growing up; you are entering into the experience of My divine dilemma. I won't try to explain it, but I do offer you My hope in it; that through your anguish and frustration, we can suffer together as you turn toward the depths of My bleeding heart. Come here. Come closer and let Me breathe fresh hope into your weary soul.

Your Turn to Respond

❖ What word or phrase are you drawn to today and why?

❖ How does the reading relate to you and your life today?

❖ What would you like to say to God?

❖ What does God want to say to you? Listen.

DAY FORTY-ONE

Then I saw yet another thing: envy fuels achievement.
All the work and skills people develop
come from their desire to be better than their neighbors.
Even this is fleeting, like trying to embrace the wind.
Ecclesiastes 4:4 (The Voice)

A Colloquy

*Don't you have a saying, "to keep up with the Joneses"? When you're honest with
yourself, what is it that inspires so much of your drive to secure your social identity?
It's not merely that you want your lawn to be as green as your neighbors. Instead,
part of you desperately craves to be great, to be recognized, admired, revered, even for
something as insignificant as your front yard.*

*If you don't discover a different center from which to work and play, everything you
do will be done in calculated reference to others; not to serve them, but to outdo and
outshine them. If you are not careful, My old friend, you may spend years, if not
decades, of your precious life seeking reassurance through this obsession to compare,
this constant monitoring of your standing to prove that you are better than others.
Then you believe that you are okay, that you've arrived. Can't you see how this
misguided pursuit will never lead you anywhere? Seeking to prove you are somebody,
always trying to outshine others is the ultimate bridge to nowhere.*

*I know it's hard for you to fully recognize, but I want you to carefully consider
the foundation of your identity. Honestly, what is it resting on? What is it really
comprised of? What do you rely on to give you a sense of substance? It's so important
for you to be clear and grounded about this, otherwise you will look to voices and
sources outside of yourself to tell you who you are.*

Your Turn to Respond

❖ What word or phrase are you drawn to today and why?

❖ How does the reading relate to you and your life today?

❖ What would you like to say to God?

❖ What does God want to say to you? Listen.

DAY FORTY-TWO

As the saying goes: The fool folds his hands
to rest and lets his flesh waste away.
And it is better to have one handful of peace
than to have two hands full of hard work
and a desire to catch the wind.
Ecclesiastes 4:5-6 (The Voice)

A Colloquy

My old friend, I don't want to discourage you from your pursuit of wisdom, but have you noticed how soon your people's conventional wisdom either fades away or is overturned by the next contrarian? For instance, haven't you heard some version of these two well-worn pieces of advice? One, from some overly serious sage, shaming the slacker into action and warning that too much R & R, too much disengagement from productivity, will lead to the inevitable and undesirable end: starvation. Haven't you noticed how conventional wisdom seeks to trigger the most base energies of shame and fear?

But later, you hear another sage contradict this commonsense advice and convincingly point out the pricelessness of a true moment of peace. The possession of a copacetic calm is trophied as an unimaginable treasure beyond all wealth and means. You are told by this one that no amount of overworking or overdoing can yield a life of simple serenity.

These conventional wisdoms and the inevitable refutations that follow may help sell more self-help books, but in the end they will wind up unsettling you more than serving you as you navigate the unique circumstances of your life.

I want you to realize that My viewpoint is not merely a composite of all the conventional wisdoms ever penned or promoted. In fact, I will more often than not offer you My unconventional wisdom that you might be freed from the many formulized illusions designed to "make life work for you." My presence will make life work for you. And even when it doesn't, you will see that in the end, all forms of mind-control, or manipulation, or the promise of reward, or threat of punishment is a mirage created by others and not by Me.

So come to Me and ask what I have to offer as you stand at the crossroads of your life. Then listen. But don't be surprised. In fact, expect to hear new words of wisdom and new ways of living.

Your Turn to Respond

❖ What word or phrase are you drawn to today and why?

❖ How does the reading relate to you and your life today?

❖ What would you like to say to God?

❖ What does God want to say to you? Listen.

DAY FORTY-THREE

I observed yet another example of something meaningless under the sun.
This is the case of a man who is all alone, without a child or a brother,
yet who works hard to gain as much wealth as he can.
But then he asks himself, "Who am I working for? Why am I giving up
so much pleasure now?" It is all so meaningless and depressing.
Ecclesiastes 4:7-8 (New Living Translation)

A Colloquy

It is so easy, and, if you can believe it, lazy, to fill up your inner emptiness with more work. Does that sound like another one of My many contradictions? Can't you see that overworking is one of the prime expressions of the laziness of your times? What do I mean by this, My old friend?

When you're lonely, when there is no one for you to offer your love and creativity to, isn't it easier to just turn to your work, to get more done, to achieve more, rather than ask yourself what you really want? My advice for you is to do everything within your power to make a family, to make friends, to make peace with joy.

Don't let work be the way you numb yourself or become an ever-ready substitute for life's pure and simple pleasures, which—never forget—are My simple pleasures. It's spiritual laziness, in fact, to deny yourself what you haven't ever taken the time or risk to admit you actually want quite badly. Do you really want to live as an affluent, yet overworked and lonely martyr? What good will that be to you in the end?

Your Turn to Respond

✦ What word or phrase are you drawn to today and why?

✦ How does the reading relate to you and your life today?

✦ What would you like to say to God?

✦ What does God want to say to you? Listen.

DAY FORTY-FOUR

Two people are better off than one, for they can help each other succeed.
If one person falls, the other can reach out and help.
But someone who falls alone is in real trouble.
Likewise, two people lying close together can keep each other warm.
But how can one be warm alone?
A person standing alone can be attacked and defeated,
but two can stand back-to-back and conquer.
Three are even better, for a triple-braided cord is not easily broken.
Ecclesiastes 4:9-12 (New Living Translation)

A Colloquy

My old friend, even though you know that I am continually with you, I have created the world in such a way that it always goes better for you—you are always stronger, less vulnerable—when you are united in heart and flesh with another.

Life becomes harder, lonelier, and more dangerous when you try to make it by yourself. Sometimes you may be tempted to go it alone. Or at other times, life circumstances beyond your control place you in that position. Try not to stay there, however, any longer than you must. But know this, I can always be that Other, especially when you find yourself untethered and alone for a season, unbound to another in love and purpose.

Your Turn to Respond

❖ What word or phrase are you drawn to today and why?

❖ How does the reading relate to you and your life today?

❖ What would you like to say to God?

❖ What does God want to say to you? Listen.

DAY FORTY-FIVE

A poor, wise youth is better off than an old,
foolish king who no longer accepts advice.
Ecclesiastes 4:13 (The Voice)

A Colloquy

Have you noticed, My old friend, that wisdom is not the exclusive attribute of the old nor foolishness the unfortunate lot of the young? There are far too many old fools who have deluded themselves into believing that they are wise simply because they have endured so many years and trials. Youth have a wisdom that their elders are ever in need of.

How many times have you heard the self-congratulatory phrase, "the greatest generation?" Don't be fooled by any gray hair who tries to play the sage based on their generational status. Honor wisdom's vitality no matter where it comes from. In fact, you need the young if many of the errors your elders have made are to be redressed. Turn your heart toward them. Open your mind to what they are saying. Are you willing to listen?

Your Turn to Respond

✦ What word or phrase are you drawn to today and why?

✦ How does the reading relate to you and your life today?

✦ What would you like to say to God?

✦ What does God want to say to you? Listen.

DAY FORTY-SIX

I saw a youth just like this start with nothing and go from rags to riches,
and I saw everyone rally to the rule of this young successor to the king.
Even so, the excitement died quickly, the throngs of people soon lost interest.
Can't you see it's only smoke? And spitting into the wind?
Ecclesiastes 4:14-16 (The Message)

A Colloquy

*There used to be a day when many young men and women, when asked what they
wanted to be when they grew up, would answer with confidence, "the President!"
Some still might answer a professional soccer player or an astronaut or a film star. All
of these positions carry a very real or imagined potential for power and influence.
When the young accomplish their dreams, the achievement is genuinely impressive.
And when these heights are reached by a young man or woman who has transcended
traumatic, difficult, impoverished beginnings, their story is truly spectacular. Some
will be elevated by well-meaning people who go on to market their story to inspire
others to do likewise.*

*And yet admiration and fame are fickle. More often than not, no matter what great
thing you've accomplished, someday, someone will come along and ridicule it. Desiring
others' respect, honor, and praise seems so natural, so virtuous, doesn't it? But realize
this: all too soon the admiration others have given you will slip through your fingers
just as surely as fine, dry sand slips through the hourglass.*

*So where do you find your reputation headed these days—on the upswing or
tumbling downward? Even though some others may exaggerate or diminish your
brand, remember that I honor you, not your aspirations. I'm totally committed to our
friendship, no matter what some others say or think of you. Never forget, I'm always
your biggest, and most faithful Friend.*

Your Turn to Respond

◈ What word or phrase are you drawn to today and why?

◈ How does the reading relate to you and your life today?

◈ What would you like to say to God?

◈ What does God want to say to you? Listen.

DAY FORTY-SEVEN

Watch your step when you enter the house of God.
Be ready to listen quietly
rather than rushing in to offer up a sacrifice to foolish people,
for they have no idea that what they do is evil.
Ecclesiastes 5:1 (The Voice)

A Colloquy

In some cultures it is customary to take off your shoes when entering a home. That holds true whether it's your own house or someone else's. That's the best way to keep the floors clean and the ambiance serene. When you clomp around, you disturb the home's peace and distract the residents from whatever they are about at the time.

In the same way, My old friend, walk in this world as if it is our shared home, one we are committed to both enjoy and protect. When you slow down and carefully listen to Mother Earth's heartbeat—her needs, her possibilities—you won't rush in and act with anxious presumption, thinking you know exactly what is called for.

Action, even so-called right action, if not preceded by careful listening will more often than not hurt rather than help. Where do you need to pay heed to this in your life?

Your Turn to Respond

✤ What word or phrase are you drawn to today and why?

✤ How does the reading relate to you and your life today?

✤ What would you like to say to God?

✤ What does God want to say to you? Listen.

DAY FORTY-EIGHT

Do not be too hasty to speak your mind before God
or too quick to make promises you won't keep,
for God is in heaven and you are on earth.
Therefore, watch your tongue; let your words be few.
For just as busyness breeds restless dreams,
so wordiness reveals the voice of a fool.
Ecclesiastes 5:2-3 (The Voice)

A Colloquy

You are learning, My old friend, that words are flimsy things. How much easier it is to say something than to do something—to follow through on what you say. In your lifetime, if you become a person who is growing in self-awareness, you will start to notice many patterns in how you relate to Me and to others with your words. You will notice just how fickle your flattering words can be at times. You will notice when you're a poser with your words, talking "big" to impress Me or others, or maybe yourself. You will discover how deceptive you can be as you hedge your bets in what you say and how you say it, forever keeping your fingers crossed behind your back.

I know you think of yourself as an honest person, and for the most part you are. And I see that when you are relaxed and at home in your own skin you speak simply, directly, and clearly. But I also want you to notice your speech when you feel less sure of yourself, or in need of something or someone. What do your words and your patterns tell you then?

Your Turn to Respond

❧ What word or phrase are you drawn to today and why?

❧ How does the reading relate to you and your life today?

❧ What would you like to say to God?

❧ What does God want to say to you? Listen.

DAY FORTY-NINE

If you make a promise to God, do not be slow to keep it;
for He takes no pleasure in fools. So do what you have promised.
In fact, it would be better not to make a vow in the first place
than to make it and not fulfill it. Do not let your mouth lead you to sin,
and do not claim before the temple messenger that your vow was a mistake.
Why should God be angry at the sound of your voice
and destroy everything you've worked hard to achieve?
Daydreaming and excessive talking are pointless and fleeting things to do,
like trying to catch hold of a breath.
What good comes from them? It is better to quietly reverence God.
Ecclesiastes 5:4-7 (The Voice)

A Colloquy

As I have been known to say, My old friend, just "let your yes be yes, and your no be no." Nothing more than that is ever required, whether you are speaking to me or someone else. Your over-promising comes from your anxious forgetfulness of who we really are to each other. When you forget who we are to each other, you will wrongly imagine that you need to win back My favor or impress Me in some way.

Forgetting all that I've shown you, all that you've experienced of My love, pierces My heart. It frustrates Me, not because I'm angry with you, but because I see so clearly where your spiritual amnesia will take you. When you forget My ongoing accessibility, My unchanging love for you, the stories you tell yourself and the schemes they inspire will strap you to an empty illusion. You may even think that your so-called personal growth, practical progress, or even spiritual transformation is what matters most to Me. Can't you see how unnecessary this all is? Simply value what you already have with Me. In a word, value us! Nothing you can say or do will ever add or subtract from our being us.

Your Turn to Respond

❖ What word or phrase are you drawn to today and why?

❖ How does the reading relate to you and your life today?

❖ What would you like to say to God?

❖ What does God want to say to you? Listen.

DAY FIFTY

Don't be surprised if you see a poor person being oppressed by the powerful
and if justice is being miscarried throughout the land.
For every official is under orders from higher up,
and matters of justice get lost in red tape and bureaucracy.
Ecclesiastes 5:8 (New Living Translation)

A Colloquy

*Power is never neutral, My old friend. Its dynamic energy-potential can be stored
like a battery, lying dormant for a season. But sooner or later it will be activated, and
once awake, the effects of power will always be seen in tangible, concrete expressions.
Then you will observe its lack of neutrality and witness particular people in specific
locations wield it, either over My beloved ones or on behalf of them.*

*There is a universal anxiety triggered by humanity's scarcity mindset. It now
permeates every aspect of society, including governments and corporations,
institutions and churches. Even your families are not immune to this worm of
contention.*

*Know this, old friend, whenever you see the poor kept down, and the privileged
refusing to practice My law of love, you can be certain that someone's personal power
is being misused for self-advancement. My leaders, however, carefully steward My
power in such a way that all prosper, especially the ones who have no power. What
power have you been given and who are you protecting or providing for with it?*

Your Turn to Respond

❖ What word or phrase are you drawn to today and why?

❖ How does the reading relate to you and your life today?

❖ What would you like to say to God?

❖ What does God want to say to you? Listen.

DAY FIFTY-ONE

Still, it is better for the land in every way
to have a king who cultivates the fields.
As the saying goes:
Those who love money will never be satisfied with money,
and those who love riches will never be happy with what they have.
This, too, is fleeting.
The more goods there are,
the more people there are to consume them.
How does any of this really benefit the owners
except they can gaze proudly on their possessions?
Sweet sleep comes to those who work hard,
regardless of how much or how little they've eaten.
But the abundance of the rich keeps them awake at night.
Ecclesiastes 5:9-12 (The Voice)

A Colloquy

You've undoubtedly heard the saying, "The love of money is the root of all evil." But have you ever considered how precisely you might measure your love of money? That's a question worth pondering, My old friend.

Have you noticed how people never seem satisfied, no matter how much money they have in their bank accounts and investments? This preoccupation of building wealth blooms quickly into an obsession, yet the inordinate attention given to it never seems to blossom into genuine and lasting joy.

Pride always feeds on comparison, and this form of pride measures one's personal value based on income and wealth. This scoring system has been carefully designed to make people feel good about themselves or bad about themselves; safe and secure or vulnerable and in danger.

No matter how much your wealth increases or what it produces, if unchecked, your exaggerated sense of need and your incessant participation in consumerism will always put you at risk—not to mention rob you of My gift of sleep.

So, My old friend, if you will learn to work with all your heart at whatever it is that brings you joy and meets your needs, you will discover that what you genuinely require is far less than you have imagined. My advice: go treat yourself to a simple, tasty meal and go to bed early. Then you will be at peace even when you hear your neighbor cursing the stock market.

Your Turn to Respond

❖ What word or phrase are you drawn to today and why?

❖ How does the reading relate to you and your life today?

❖ What would you like to say to God?

❖ What does God want to say to you? Listen.

DAY FIFTY-TWO

There is another serious problem I have seen under the sun.
Hoarding riches harms the saver.
Money is put into risky investments that turn sour, and everything is lost.
In the end, there is nothing left to pass on to one's children.
We all come to the end of our lives as naked and
empty-handed as on the day we were born.
We can't take our riches with us.
And this, too, is a very serious problem.
People leave this world no better off than when they came.
All their hard work is for nothing—like working for the wind.
Throughout their lives, they live under a cloud—
frustrated, discouraged, and angry.
Ecclesiastes 5:13-17 (New Living Translation)

A Colloquy

If you were to take a snapshot of the affluent when they are at the top of their game, their lot in life seems absolutely secure. And for a period of time, financial prosperity does afford a certain limited form of protection. But life is more like a full-length movie than a still shot.

I have made a very narrow gate through which all must pass, My old friend. I have made it so that eventually death, your death, will take everything from you, down to the very clothes on your back. It should cause you to ask what all your striving and straining is really for, now that you lay flat on your back, taking in that one last breath.

Does it seem unfair that at life's finish line, regardless of how well off you are, or how well you performed, everyone in the end loses everything? I understand how this fact can darken your mood, leaving only a sour taste in your mouth, even toward Me. But since this fact is inevitable, how will you ready yourself? Could you begin practicing, even now, to say goodbye to everything you love.

Your Turn to Respond

◆ What word or phrase are you drawn to today and why?

◆ How does the reading relate to you and your life today?

◆ What would you like to say to God?

◆ What does God want to say to you? Listen.

DAY FIFTY-THREE

Then it dawned on me that this is good and proper:
to eat and drink and find the good in all the toil that we undertake
under the sun during the few days God has given,
for this is our lot in life.
Also, God gives wealth, possessions, and power to enjoy those things,
and He allows them to accept their lot in life and to enjoy hard work.
This is God's gift.
For people like this have no time to despair over life
because God keeps them so busy with a deep-seated joy.
Ecclesiastes 5:18-20 (The Voice)

A Colloquy

My old friend, you and I have walked together long enough for you to know what brings Me pleasure. Give your full attention to the simple goodness of life. It brings Me such joy to share with you good food, sweet drink, and creation's bounty for your enjoyment and satisfaction.

It's all a gift, however, that you must participate in—planting, watering, and harvesting. But that doesn't make it any less of a gift. Even the expenditure of your strength and energy can be deeply fulfilling if you view it as I do.

It may seem at times like I am disparaging all wealth and all possessions and all forms of power. I am not. Rather, I am simply reminding you to keep your priorities straight. And the first order of all My priorities is to remain actively present as you participate in My joyfully creative work in the world. If you remember this, you will have no interest in complaining about how bad the world is. Rather, you will give yourself completely to tackling what's right in front of you.

Your Turn to Respond

✤ What word or phrase are you drawn to today and why?

✤ How does the reading relate to you and your life today?

✤ What would you like to say to God?

✤ What does God want to say to you? Listen.

DAY FIFTY-FOUR

I have seen another injustice under the sun,
one that is a real burden upon humanity.
Sometimes God gives money, possessions, and even honor,
so that we have everything a person might desire; nothing is lacking.
But then, for reasons God only knows,
God does not allow him to enjoy the good gifts.
Rather, a stranger ends up enjoying them. This, too, is fleeting;
it's a sickening evil.
If a person has one hundred children and lives for many years
but finds no satisfaction in all of the good things that life brings
and in the end doesn't have a proper burial,
I say that it would be better if that person had been stillborn
because the stillborn arrives in a fleeting breath
and then goes nameless into the darkness mourned by no one
and buried in an unmarked grave.
Though the child never sees the sun or knows anything,
it still had more rest than the person who cannot enjoy what he has.
Even if a person were to live one thousand years twice over,
but could find no satisfaction,
don't we all end up going to the same place?
Ecclesiastes 6:1-6 (The Message)

A Colloquy

I'm sure you've heard the song by the Rolling Stones, "I Can't Get No Satisfaction."
That title seems to be a fitting byline for your culture's carefully orchestrated
psychology of dissatisfaction; an ethos that's always quietly humming in the
background?

There are so many people in the world who have everything anyone could dream of—
who even attribute their blessed lives to Me. How is it that they find themselves at a
complete loss to genuinely enjoy what actually comes from My hand? I want to satisfy
everyone's desires with good things. Can you believe that, My old friend? But there are
so many powerful forces at work in your personality that conspire to rob you of My
physical, spiritual and psychological blessings.

You can easily understand someone who has next to nothing being restless in their dissatisfaction. We could even call this a "holy dissatisfaction." But how do you account for the one who has everything, yet who is unable to experience stable and lasting contentment, let alone the genuine fulfillment that could be theirs? What's fueling your discontentment these days? Can you name it?

Your Turn to Respond

❖ What word or phrase are you drawn to today and why?

❖ How does the reading relate to you and your life today?

❖ What would you like to say to God?

❖ What does God want to say to you? Listen.

DAY FIFTY-FIVE

All people spend their lives scratching for food,
but they never seem to have enough.
So are wise people really better off than fools?
Do poor people gain anything by being wise
and knowing how to act in front of others?
Enjoy what you have rather than desiring what you don't have.
Just dreaming about nice things is meaningless—
like chasing the wind.
Ecclesiastes 6:7-9 (New Living Translation)

A Colloquy

Do you really believe that the sweat and toil expended in work is for the sole purpose of putting food in your belly, My old friend? If that's all, then I understand why your labor is so empty and unsatisfying. Approaching your life's work that way diminishes what you do to a necessary, yet regrettable transaction. But you will find sooner or later that all transactional living doesn't satisfy the hunger of your soul.

Is the well-spoken, well-dressed salesperson, always on the hustle, really any better off than the customer who walks in the door with a maxed-out credit card? In the end, those who profit from knowing how the world works, as well as the poor losers you see on street corners, never develop a palate to taste My soul food. My nourishing abundance can be found in every meal or morsel set before you, whether served on a humble or elegant table setting. Do you know or have you really considered what it is you really want, what you are really working so hard for? Learn to enjoy what you have rather than indulging in the bread of dissatisfaction. This will be more than enough reward for all your good labor.

Your Turn to Respond

❖ What word or phrase are you drawn to today and why?

❖ How does the reading relate to you and your life today?

❖ What would you like to say to God?

❖ What does God want to say to you? Listen.

DAY FIFTY-SIX

Whatever exists has already been named.
Human nature, as it is with its strengths and limitations, is already known.
So no one dares to dispute with One so much stronger than he.
Ecclesiastes 6:10 (The Voice)

A Colloquy

Look around you, My old friend. What do you see? Depending on where you are standing or the direction you turn your head, have you noticed how everything has a name, a word, a label linked to it? Each symbol of your language is filled with countless images and associations. For instance, when you hear the word "box" what comes to mind? Confinement? A beautifully wrapped present? Two men throwing punches at one another?

When all combined, these strands of your interconnected experiences, memories, and feelings make it nearly impossible to truly see something or someone in their unique particularity.

Even the complex dimensions of your own inner being, your personality and proclivities, have been given labels. Words like introversion or will or ego all point to some intangible dimension of the human experience. But even when named, they still seem to remain a mystery to you, just beyond your mind's ability to grasp.

Look to Me and I will help you see beneath all labels, categories, and surface appearances. And why does this matter? To strengthen and sharpen your proficiency in the art of discernment, you simply must develop a capacity to see and understand beyond all the blinding labels you have been given. If you stay close to Me and watch me, My divine perspective, which is free from all these depersonalizing generalizations, will rub off on you. It will empower you to authentically pursue what you really care about. And your discernment will know no limits.

Your Turn to Respond

◆ What word or phrase are you drawn to today and why?

◆ How does the reading relate to you and your life today?

◆ What would you like to say to God?

◆ What does God want to say to you? Listen.

DAY FIFTY-SEVEN

The more the words,
the less the meaning,
and how does that profit anyone?
Ecclesiastes 6:11 (New International Version)

A Colloquy

A single word; a short, heart-felt phrase. Most of the time, My old friend, that's all that is needed.

Have you ever stopped to think about all the words you have spoken over the years of your life? Some people seem to never stop talking, while others seem to barely speak more than two or three words at a time. When you weigh the quality, the heart of your communication, you will find less is more.

The people around you are trying to breathe, they are trying to be. So don't interrupt their living with empty words. Save your breath. If your words are flavored with love, joy and truth, volume of output is irrelevant. It's not so much that the squeaky wheel gets oiled — no, it simply gets ignored. Enter into My rhythm, the rhythm of grace-filled speech. Speak in time with the tempo and the tone I use.

Your Turn to Respond

✦ What word or phrase are you drawn to today and why?

✦ How does the reading relate to you and your life today?

✦ What would you like to say to God?

✦ What does God want to say to you? Listen.

DAY FIFTY-EIGHT

For who knows the best way for us to live
during the few days of our fleeting lives?
After all, we pass through them like shadows.
For who can say what will happen
under the sun after we are gone?
Ecclesiastes 6:12 (The Voice)

A Colloquy

Does your life have meaning? How would it sit with you if that's for Me to say, and not you, My old friend?

Does a tree's shadow have meaning? Do moss or mushrooms have meaning? Your life is like a shady spot whose transience is ever apparent yet does not diminish its meaningfulness. As night reappears, the shade disappears. The shadow seems to dissolve into the darkness. But look up in the morning—the tree is still standing. Because of its presence, the new day will again be full of soft, lovely shadows and subtle, cool shade.

Have you considered that it may actually be less about whether your life matters or has meaning and more about your recognizing and honoring that which is personally meaningful to you and to others?

Your Turn to Respond

✦ What word or phrase are you drawn to today and why?

✦ How does the reading relate to you and your life today?

✦ What would you like to say to God?

✦ What does God want to say to you? Listen.

DAY FIFTY-NINE

A good name is better than fine perfume
Ecclesiastes 7:1a (New International Version)

A Colloquy

When I hear your name spoken, My old friend, it still makes me smile. Your name becomes richer, more beautiful to Me and others, as you settle into your unique interior landscape along with your particular exterior geography. Like a fine wine, you open to life's subtle elements around you and they begin to flavor your life with intriguing, complex structures. Then, when you are remembered or addressed by name, a fresh burst of YOU is released into the world. We love your name because we love you.

I will help guard your name, if you'll let me, and make the mere thought of you a blessing, a salve. Then, when you are spoken of, it will be as if I, too, am being spoken of. Unfortunately, My name has been sullied. It has become for many an epithet of derision and abusive projections. I'm not sure My name can be unlinked from the evil that has been promulgated by religious zealots. I'm a realist, you know.

So in the short run, your good and beautiful name will have to do. It will help to heal others who are disgusted with or afraid of My name. When these frightened, angry ones catch the beauty of your fragrance, My hope is that they will turn aside and begin their pilgrimage back home to the center of My Nameless Presence.

Your Turn to Respond

✦ What word or phrase are you drawn to today and why?

✦ How does the reading relate to you and your life today?

✦ What would you like to say to God?

✦ What does God want to say to you? Listen.

DAY SIXTY

The day you die is better than the day you were born.
In the same way, it is better to go to a funeral than a celebration.
Why? because death is the end of life's journey,
and the living should always take that to heart.
Ecclesiastes 7:1b-2 (The Voice)

A Colloquy

What do you think about dying, My old friend? For that matter, what are your thoughts about your birth? How do you really feel about both your death and life's ending, as well as your birth and life's beginning?

You're not alone if you feel an uncomfortable resistance to contemplate either your arrival or your departure. But consider this: your life has been filled with countless little birthings and little dyings. Haven't you somehow survived them all up to this point? I am with you in each of your celebrations, as well as in each and every burial.

Depending on how hard your life feels at the moment, you might even consider the ending of your life as better than its beginning. I understand how all these sorrowful, painful losses can make you feel that way. But contrary to certain theological misconceptions of death's origin, I have made the ending as well as the beginning. It is not human failing or misdeeds that have given birth to this natural phenomenon. I have made both life and death. So fear not, I am with you in it all. In the meantime, live fully all of life's little births and seek Me in each little death. For neither your beginning, nor your ending is My final word to you.

Your Turn to Respond

✦ What word or phrase are you drawn to today and why?

✦ How does the reading relate to you and your life today?

✦ What would you like to say to God?

✦ What does God want to say to you? Listen.

DAY SIXTY-ONE

Sorrow beats foolish laughter;
embracing sadness somehow gladdens our hearts.
A wise heart is well acquainted with grief,
but a foolish heart seeks only pleasure's company.
Ecclesiastes 7:3-4 (The Voice)

A Colloquy

I don't make the same split, the same judgment you do, My old friend. Both your laughter and your tears find a home in Me. Some people, unfortunately, resent other people's joy, fixated and trapped by their own losses and sorrows. They find grief to be a thief, prowling around any of life's unlocked windows, seeking to steal its sweetness. Their cynicism comes to define and confine them.

I want to heal this split in you. Above all, I have made you for joy. My joy over you is your strength. My joy directed toward you reminds you of how glad I am to be with you. Therefore this joy we share will always reemerge as the most natural pursuit in your life. I never intend to deprive you of it, even when you are in the midst of great pain and great loss.

So loosen your grip. Great joy and great sorrow can co-exist. For I have also made you with a capacity to grieve. I am glad to be with you in the depths as well as the heights. Feel all your feelings. You won't fall into an endless, black pit. Even in your darkest times, I will diligently be at work to bring to the surface some of My richest gifts, treasures which could never be mined in the light of day. There you will find Me in ways you have not yet imagined. There we will share many intimate tears that only can be dried after they have been cried in communion. This too, paradoxically, is My great joy.

Your Turn to Respond

❖ What word or phrase are you drawn to today and why?

❖ How does the reading relate to you and your life today?

❖ What would you like to say to God?

❖ What does God want to say to you? Listen.

DAY SIXTY-TWO

Better to be criticized by a wise person
than to be praised by a fool.
A fool's laughter is quickly gone,
like thorns crackling in a fire.
This also is meaningless.
Ecclesiastes 7:5-6 (New Living Translation)

A Colloquy

Have you noticed, My old friend, how most of the so-called wise seem so serious, so intense, so uptight? Theirs is a harsh wisdom that is forever correcting faults. Always looking down from on high toward others.

On the other hand, those often viewed as foolish or immature seem to be light-hearted, frivolous fun-lovers, those you'd want to invite to a party.

These two extremes seem hopelessly locked in a never-ending contest. So where do you land? Are you too adult to let go and enjoy yourself? Are you too childish to buckle down and contribute meaningfully to the world?

It makes Me wonder how you see Me? Can you see in Me both the Holy Fool as well as the Laughing Sage? Or are you too grown-up to hear Me whistling a silly love song?

Your Turn to Respond

❖ What word or phrase are you drawn to today and why?

❖ How does the reading relate to you and your life today?

❖ What would you like to say to God?

❖ What does God want to say to you? Listen.

DAY SIXTY-THREE

Brutality stupefies even the wise
and destroys the strongest heart.
Ecclesiastes 7:7 (The Message)

A Colloquy

My old friend, it saddens My heart that certain hard, stringent portrayals of Me still persist, making Me out to be an oppressor; Someone always opposed to mankind's humanity, always demanding more than is reasonable, never content with any lack of perfection or results.

No wonder so many of My children turn away from this form of religion. I'd turn away, too. In fact, I have turned away and forsaken any system, religion, or spirituality which seeks to control through dominance.

Don't curry favors with power if you desire your heart to remain free and uncontaminated. You can bet that even the gifts and offerings that are brought to a church or the cause of your choice, if they are intended as a means of pleasing someone who has power, will be a thinly veiled act of bribery or appeasement, and not a heartfelt expression of love.

Your Turn to Respond

❧ What word or phrase are you drawn to today and why?

❧ How does the reading relate to you and your life today?

❧ What would you like to say to God?

❧ What does God want to say to you? Listen.

DAY SIXTY-FOUR

Having the last word is better than having the first.
Ecclesiastes 7:8a (The Voice)

A Colloquy

It's so good to initiate a conversation, isn't it, My old friend? I love the words you bring that open up and invite an exchange of heart and ideas. But in the rough and tumble of any meaningful relationship or exchange, things can be spoken that would have been better left unspoken. Temperatures can rise and arguments marshaled. And so, don't forget, last words are lasting words. They ring as either harmonious chimes or reverberate as an alarm bell.

Your final expressions are best received when heavily seasoned with understanding, appreciation, respect, forgiveness, and joyful hope. So when you say goodbye, let your final words be a blessing, spoken either in your heart or with your lips—or better, both. As you preview your day and those you will speak to, what are your hopes for your interactions? Name them one by one. How might you seek to bless them?

Your Turn to Respond

❖ What word or phrase are you drawn to today and why?

❖ How does the reading relate to you and your life today?

❖ What would you like to say to God?

❖ What does God want to say to you? Listen.

DAY SIXTY-FIVE

Patience will benefit you more than pride.
Do not be quick to anger,
for anger sits comfortably in the lap of fools.
Ecclesiastes 7:8b-9 (New Living Translation)

A Colloquy

Have you lived long enough, My old friend, to observe My patient love? I never lose hope, never lose My temper, even as I tolerate the intolerable. Consider how old the universe is or the age of your planet and its evolving journey. For that matter, observe the scope of the human species and its history. I am comfortable with eons of non-human and human history, not rushing anything. So what's a few days or weeks or years?

Pride will forever make you impatient and angry with anyone who does not cooperate with your vision of how the world should be. Because of this, it's so easy for you to think of Me as being driven by My power, by My strength, by some misguided understanding of My divine right to glory and the conformity of all creation to My wishes. If that were true, I would never have begun this humble experiment of Creative Love.

Am I ever angry, you wonder. Yes, but not as you imagine, not as you have experienced in others. There is an intensity—a ferocity—found in My Love that can easily be misunderstood. But the burning furnace you find in Me originates not in My oppositional nature or some presumed Divine Ego trip. The heat from My heart blazes and burns only with Love. And you? What are you feeling especially intense about today? Is it formed in the furnace of Love or is it being fueled from some other source?

Your Turn to Respond

✦ What word or phrase are you drawn to today and why?

✦ How does the reading relate to you and your life today?

✦ What would you like to say to God?

✦ What does God want to say to you? Listen.

DAY SIXTY-SIX

Don't long for "the good old days." This is not wise.

Ecclesiastes 7:10 (New Living Translation)

A Colloquy

At some point in your life, My old friend, you will ask the question, "Will I ever be happy again?" Or "What happened to the good old days?" You've likely whispered that question during times when all the sweetness, all the glimmer and glow of sunnier days has evaporated, leaving you with little to cling to, little to hope for, and nothing to savor.

I welcome this honest prayer, these questions of sadness and despondency. It may seem sometimes better to just put on a happy face. Or you might wrongly consider voicing your grief-riddled questions as evidence of your lack of faith or some other pious judgment.

Wisdom never avoids an uncomfortable or unanswerable truth. So bring all your questions to Me, no matter how irreverent or foolish they seem. Just remember, some answers take a long, long time to come. And when they do arrive you may find that many of the feelings you once had are now forgotten, and what has come to pass has ushered in a new chapter filled with its own blessings and conundrums. Think for a moment, and be honest: What questions are you carrying that you'd like to bring to Me? I'd like to hear them. I'd like to engage with all that really matters to you.

Your Turn to Respond

✦ What word or phrase are you drawn to today and why?

✦ How does the reading relate to you and your life today?

✦ What would you like to say to God?

✦ What does God want to say to you? Listen.

DAY SIXTY-SEVEN

Wisdom is even better when you have money.
Both are a benefit as you go through life.
Wisdom and money can get you almost anything,
but only wisdom can save your life.
Ecclesiastes 7:11-12 (New Living Translation)

A Colloquy

I am a God who believes in the simple preposition, "and." How I wish that all My children would not only learn to use it but become a believer in it. For instance, I hold both life and death, night and day not as opposites, but as necessary complements. Of course they are radically different, and yet one should not be mistakenly elevated as good or right while the other is wrong or evil.

I say all this in light of our conversations, My old friend. I don't want to confuse you when you hear Me say that having both material means, and a spiritually wise mind is of immense value. Each day brings fresh opportunities and new challenges, circumstances in which every spiritual and material resource given to you can assist in protecting and providing for you and those in your care.

Someday, however, your material resources will fail you; they will be unable to preserve whatever you've carefully accumulated. At that point, draw upon our history together. You can still be guided by your seasoned, wise heart. This spiritual wisdom you now have can do for you what no material advantage can make up for.

Do you wonder what it is that wisdom can do? You'll have to wait and find out when you're stymied. But somehow between a rock and a hard place, you'll discover, My old friend, the shimmering brilliance of a third-way, invisible until now, but made available by not collapsing "and" into "but." Are you willing and open to consider that now? Are you patient enough to seek and wait for a third way—a way you have not yet imagined?

Your Turn to Respond

❖ What word or phrase are you drawn to today and why?

❖ How does the reading relate to you and your life today?

❖ What would you like to say to God?

❖ What does God want to say to you? Listen.

DAY SIXTY-EIGHT

Take a good look at God's work.
Who could simplify and reduce Creation's curves and angles
to a plain straight line?
Ecclesiastes 7:13 (The Message)

A Colloquy

I want you to consider My work, My workmanship. It's all around you. It's even in you. What do you notice, My old friend? What do you believe about My work and workmanship? Take a good hard and honest look. What do you actually observe?

If you really look at what I've done and what I'm doing, you'll see that I'm no Cosmic Perfectionist. I am not a Being, always restless and wrestling, with some divine ideal. I love to work with what is. I create both with and in reality. Whether something is crooked or straight, I find beauty in the twists and turns of it all.

Sometimes you think you know better than Me how things should be, don't you? Then, you set out on a program (your program) of straightening everything out. Can't you see that's not what I'm all about? The only perfection I care about is perfect love. When love is perfect, everything and everyone is more than okay, however it is. So, relax in love and learn to enjoy all the surprising, diverse, irregular people or things around you. I like it that way. I like you that way!

So what about you? Is there someone in your life you still hold to an unrealistic standard and your expectations block a free expression of your love?

Your Turn to Respond

✤ What word or phrase are you drawn to today and why?

✤ How does the reading relate to you and your life today?

✤ What would you like to say to God?

✤ What does God want to say to you? Listen.

DAY SIXTY-NINE

When times are good, enjoy them and be happy.
When times are bad, think about this:
God makes both good and bad times,
so that no one really knows what is coming next.
Ecclesiastes 7:14 (The Voice)

A Colloquy

Do you really think you can predict your future, My old friend? Or know what tomorrow or next week or next year will bring? You think you can. And in some cases, it's possible to know some things about your life and its future. For instance, when winter comes, you know you will need extra food stored up and a good source of heat and protection from the cold. Or when the blossoms are heavy on the apple tree, you can expect a fruitful harvest in late summer. But even then, you can't know with absolute certainty that a mold won't set in to spoil your foodstuffs or a late spring frost will arrive to wither the apple blossoms.

I've not made our world like a mechanism, always churning out ease and comfort in any and all directions. Nor have I created it so that it centers around you and your kind, subservient to your every need or wish. The world, in fact, is too real for that and won't be conscripted to collaborate with humanities narcissism or egocentricity. It's a fluid, mysteriously dynamic system. I have made it so.

But don't be overly anxious when things are pleasant for you, always worrying when the next shoe will drop. Rejoice! Be glad! Stay present as long as you can. But equally, never be shocked or caught off guard if the bottom falls out and you find yourself in free fall.

Remember, I am with you just as much in the good times as I am in the bad times. Not only am I with you, I'm also experiencing the joy and the pain of it all right alongside you. The only prediction you can make in this world with 100% accuracy is this: I am in everything I've made, and I will never desert you, even if everything in life turns sour, or dangerous, or even evil. How does that strike you? Is there something more that you want or need from Me? Tell Me about it. I understand how vulnerable you feel in the situation you find yourself.

Your Turn to Respond

✤ What word or phrase are you drawn to today and why?

✤ How does the reading relate to you and your life today?

✤ What would you like to say to God?

✤ What does God want to say to you? Listen.

DAY SEVENTY

In the fleeting time I have lived on this earth,
I have seen just about everything:
the good dying in their goodness
and the wicked living to a ripe old age.
So my advice?
Do not act overly righteous, and do not
think yourself wiser than others.
Why go and ruin yourself?
But do not be too wicked or foolish either.
Why die before it's your time?
Grasp both sides of things
and keep the two in balance;
for anyone who fears God
won't give in to the extremes.
Ecclesiastes 7:15-18 (The Voice)

A Colloquy

Notice how these phrases hit you, My old friend. An untimely death. An unlived life. Taking too many foolish risks. Taking the moral high road. Do they paralyze you? Or provide you with guidance?

How can you navigate extremes like these so that you don't die physically before your time, or live too long in a vapid, unimaginative state of repetitive safeness?

Don't hold back from living or at least trying to live your life all the way up to its furthest boundaries. How will you even know where these boundaries are unless you live from time to time in a way that may even take you beyond them? Haven't you noticed that being a goody-two-shoes doesn't insure you will live longer than some so-called "fool" who runs wildly through the snow barefoot? Look around you: good people die prematurely while at the same time notorious spendthrifts live to be 100! Grasp the energy of both the foolish, wise youth and the wise, old fool! Resist the impulse to always play the middle. Consider where it is you want to land. Playing it safe or playing to win.

Your Turn to Respond

❖ What word or phrase are you drawn to today and why?

❖ How does the reading relate to you and your life today?

❖ What would you like to say to God?

❖ What does God want to say to you? Listen.

DAY SEVENTY-ONE

Wisdom is more powerful to a wise person
than 10 rulers in a city.
There is not a righteous person on earth
who always does good and never sins.
Don't take to heart all that people say;
eventually you may hear your servant curse you.
And face it, your heart has overheard
how often you've cursed others.
I have tested all of these sayings against wisdom.
I promised myself, "I will become wise,"
but wisdom kept its distance.
True wisdom remains elusive;
its profound mysteries are remote.
Who can discover it?
Ecclesiastes 7:19-24 (The Voice)

A Colloquy

*Have you noticed, My old friend, how much unsolicited advice is offered in My name
by those who make a living pontificating on their so-called great pearls of wisdom?
There's even an entire section of the Hebrew scriptures filled with shaming "shoulds"
and "shouldn'ts."*

*Don't be fooled, and don't become wisdom's nag or wisdom's slave. In fact, most of
what is dispensed as someone's well-meaning advice is not true wisdom. Wisdom is
deep. Wisdom is hidden. Wisdom is dark. And wisdom is more often than not counter
intuitive.*

*So, if you want a "how-to manual," buy a new product engineered by professional
gadget makers. My wisdom is not a catalog of divine advice giving. My wisdom is a
hidden well that confounds without seeking to control; that lures the heart without
providing a map; that loves the quest regardless of the means or the destination.
So don't try to co-opt My wisdom for your own purposes, no matter how well meaning.
It doesn't work that way; life doesn't work that way; and I certainly don't work that
way. Can you accept this?*

Your Turn to Respond

❖ What word or phrase are you drawn to today and why?

❖ How does the reading relate to you and your life today?

❖ What would you like to say to God?

❖ What does God want to say to you? Listen.

DAY SEVENTY-TWO

So I turned and dedicated my heart to knowing more, to digging deeper,
to searching harder for wisdom and the reasons things are as they are.
I applied myself to understanding the connection
between wickedness and folly, between folly and madness.
Ecclesiastes 7:25 (The Voice)

A Colloquy

*Have you noticed, My old friend, how your mind is always seeking answers?
Searching for dots and their invisible connections? Trying to penetrate the
impenetrable with the simplistic logic of cause and effect. Life is more mysterious than
equations or formulae.*

*Wisdom does not necessarily make one wise, just as folly does not always lead you
away from Me. Have you noticed how many leaders, whether spiritual or secular,
begin with humble hearts, only to end up looking like fools? In the same way, how
often does it take the wheels coming off from personal, relational, or moral failure to
actually bring you to Me?*

*It's not an explanation, another theory, idea, or doctrine that you need. It's simpler
than that. Wisdom's foundation is Me, My presence always with you, whether life
seems absurd or straight forward. So learn to relax the defenses of your mind, so that
you can be gently present to all your states of being, "warts and all" as the saying goes.
Loosen your attachment to the certainties you've acquired and watch what kind of
person you become. Perhaps you'd better recognize yourself in Me.*

*Remember, the wisdom that is Mine does crazy things sometimes. I do crazy things
sometimes! Love will often be judged by the anxious as foolish or even mad. Mad love
is a thing, you know. Do you find yourself drawn to join Me in this mad adventure of
love? If you're ready, I'm anxious to get started. Where do you think we should begin?*

Your Turn to Respond

♦ What word or phrase are you drawn to today and why?

♦ How does the reading relate to you and your life today?

♦ What would you like to say to God?

♦ What does God want to say to you? Listen.

DAY SEVENTY-THREE

Along this journey, I discovered something
more bitter than death—a seductive woman.
Her heart is a trap and net. Her hands shackle your wrists.
Those who seek to please God will escape her clutches,
but sinners will be caught in her trap. Look at this!
After investigating the matter thoroughly
to find out why things are as they are,
I realize that although I kept on searching,
I have not found what I am looking for.
Only one man in a thousand have I found,
but I could not find a single woman
among all of these who knows this.
Here is what I have figured out:
God made humanity for good,
but we humans go out
and scheme our way into trouble.
Ecclesiastes 7:26-29 (The Voice)

A Colloquy

*There you go again, My old friend, seeking some moral strategy to make life work.
Even sadder, a stringent formula to keep Me happy. And then to top it all off, you place
the blame on someone else. Worse than that, you've related to My daughters, made in
my very likeness, in the most demeaning, objectifying way.*

*The allure and beauty of women is never a problem to confront or avoid. Can't you see
how your patriarchy has manipulated you to place all the blame on the vulnerable?
Instead of extending protection and dignity to those who have been misused and
devalued, you blindly malign them. Don't you understand their desperation, their
feeling of having no choice but to collaborate with the arrogant systems of power that
abuse them?*

*At times I think you have learned very little from Me. You keep saying you want to
understand why things are the way they are. Yet after I explain it, you quickly fall
back into your small mental ruts and dig into your places of privilege, all the while
diminishing others whose needs and struggles to survive still escape you.*

Your idea of what's good is often miles apart from Mine. Your patriarchal systems are corrupt because they are fixated on an illusion, a mirage of some grand idea of perfection, of rightness, of the way things should be. Give it up, My old friend. Your moral restlessness is not needed by Me and certainly never helpful to others.
Pay attention to your moral indignations, My old friend. Then ask Me about who they are designed to serve and why they offend you so much.

Your Turn to Respond

✦ What word or phrase are you drawn to today and why?

✦ How does the reading relate to you and your life today?

✦ What would you like to say to God?

✦ What does God want to say to you? Listen.

DAY SEVENTY-FOUR

Who is like the wise man?
And who knows the interpretation of a matter?
A man's wisdom illumines his face,
and causes his stern face to beam.

Ecclesiastes 8:1 (The Amplified Bible)

A Colloquy

You are right, My old friend. To find a wise, sensitive, insightful person can feel like a lifelong search for buried treasure. They are out there, and when you are introduced to one of them it's a unique thrill, isn't it? So many you pass by or interact with have become dull, indifferent to life. All the sparkle they once had has sadly been exchanged in a bad bargain for what has become a meager existence.

What about you? Why don't you take a moment now, right now, where you're seated. Look up. Tilt your head back and drink in what you see. Now, soften your gaze. Let the corners of your mouth curve up into a gentle smile. How do you feel? Can you feel the quiet shift? Do you notice, even for an instant, your incessant worries slipping away? Can you sense a slight, new stirring in your mind and heart? A life affirming spark warming your present awareness?

Wisdom requires wakefulness. It grows in your active embodiment in the world. Don't believe you can reason your way into wisdom or wisdom's fruits. No. Reverse your seeking and allow the movements of your body to lead you back to your heart and forward into My nearness. Is this new for you—to find Me and My ways not only in your mind and your thoughts, but also in your body? Don't be timid to engage your physical experience in your body as a rich, ever-present source of divine knowing.

Your Turn to Respond

✦ What word or phrase are you drawn to today and why?

✦ How does the reading relate to you and your life today?

✦ What would you like to say to God?

✦ What does God want to say to you? Listen.

DAY SEVENTY-FIVE

Obey the king since you vowed to God that you would.
Don't try to avoid doing your duty, and don't stand with those who plot evil,
for the king can do whatever he wants.
His command is backed by great power. No one can resist or question it.
Those who obey him will not be punished.
Ecclesiastes 8:2-5 (New Living Translation)

A Colloquy

Have you not noticed that along with an experience of one's personal privilege comes a heightened attachment to the pleasures of power? The greater one's self-estimation, the greater one's conscious or unconscious exercise of control through intimidation or manipulation.

There is no divinely ordained government or power structure, My old friend. Have you not noticed how those who create these political systems all seem to appeal to a higher power ("In God we trust"). Then they go on to govern in ways that are almost always guided by "national interests," which is actually only self-interest writ large? Even Israel could not resist conceiving of their unique identity in a way that eventually became corrupted arrogance and self-righteousness. Any attempt to immortalize the hierarchical structures of the past or present in My name is both misleading and misguided.

If you choose, you can cower and fawn over those who claim to have been given special status. But in doing so, you will forfeit the precious gift of your freedom. For you see, Mine is a kingdom unlike all other monarchies ("the rule of one"). Mine is a round table of mutual regard. Any other portrayal of Me is a hoax and a fraud, so don't collaborate in any way with these systems of control, whether large or small. To live this way requires that you stand with My strength, as well as strength from your inmost being. Then you can confidently consider questions like these. Who do you need to resist and stand up to? How can you stand free? With whom do you need to stand beside, as an equal?

Your Turn to Respond

◆ What word or phrase are you drawn to today and why?

◆ How does the reading relate to you and your life today?

◆ What would you like to say to God?

◆ What does God want to say to you? Listen.

DAY SEVENTY-SIX

Yes, there is a time and a way to deal with every situation,
even when a person's troubles are on the rise.
For no one knows what is going to happen,
so who can warn him before it does?
No one can master the wind and contain it—it blows as it will.
No one has power over the day of death—it comes as it will.
No soldier is discharged in the heat of battle,
and certainly wickedness will not release those entangled in it.
Ecclesiastes 8:6-8 (The Voice)

A Colloquy

Too often, My old friend, you have swung as a pendulum between bitter despair and heroic optimism. I'm trying to show you another way, a third way, My way: the way of faith, hope, and love. Perhaps then this endless and exhausting cycle can be broken.

You wrongly believe that if you could only predict, and therefore control life and death, then everything would be as it should be. You must find—and the sooner the better— that faith, hope, and love thrive best in conditions of not knowing and not controlling.

The future is truly open. Can you believe that? I know as much as can be known, and yet I don't know with absolute certainty what precisely lies ahead for you or others. I know that shocks you, maybe even offends your theological sensibilities. But I have created your life, along with the reality of this cosmos, with a range of possibilities, not absolute certainties and predictabilities. I, too, move in My own way along the same path of faith, hope and love.

The beauty of it all is that faith, hope, and love rewrite life's possibilities again and again and again. The result is nothing less than miraculous; your story infused with deep, pervasive veins of grace, rather than the predictably bland logic of human laws.

A third way? Your three sisters—Faith, Hope, and Love—will show you the road. They will show you how to walk it and what to pay attention to. With them, skipping along beside you, who knows what might come about?

Where do you want to move forward with Faith and with Hope today? And how might Love guide and direct your steps when you're uncertain?

Your Turn to Respond

✦ What word or phrase are you drawn to today and why?

✦ How does the reading relate to you and your life today?

✦ What would you like to say to God?

✦ What does God want to say to you? Listen.

DAY SEVENTY-SEVEN

I have witnessed all of this as I have focused my attention on
all that is done under the sun:
whenever one person oppresses another to lift himself up,
it only hurts him in the end.
I have witnessed the wicked buried with honor
because during their lifetimes they would go in and out of the temple,
and soon their crimes were forgotten
in the very city where they committed them.
This, too, is fleeting.
When the penalty for a crime is not carried out quickly,
then people start scheming to commit their own crimes.
Although a wicked person commits a hundred sins and still lives a long life,
I am confident it will go better for those who worship the one True God
and stand in awe before Him,
and it will not go well for the wicked
nor will their days grow long like evening shadows
because they do not stand in awe of God.
Here is another example of the fleeting nature of our world:
there are just people who get what the wicked deserve;
there are wicked people who get what the just deserve.
I say this, too, is fleeting.
Ecclesiastes 8:9-14 (The Voice)

A Colloquy

*Have you noticed, My old friend, how you judge every crime that you've witnessed?
Whether subtly or not, you tell yourself you are capable of objectivity and able to
divine who should be punished and what their sentence should be.*

*You have learned to find deep satisfaction in those stories where the good guys win,
and the bad guys suffer. But life has not evolved along the arc of that script, has it?
How simple it would be if that were the case.*

*If My morality were simply a legal code, you might like its clean lines and boundaries,
along with its swift and tangible repercussions. That is until you or someone you loved
strays a bit too far from the straight and narrow and faces sobering consequences.*

I know it can be maddening, but this moral ambiguity which seems like a sloppy experiment, devoid of the consistent rules of cause and effect, will train you in compassion and understanding.

I'm modeling for you how to gaze at everyone with love, including the wickedly despicable. And isn't that really how you want Me to see each and every one of you? Would you really want to live in a world where everything is so tightly controlled that faith, hope, and love are unnecessary? My world, the real world, is one where these three virtues are essential not because of the absence of evil, but because of its presence.

So give up trying to play the junior prosecutor and learn to be with Me in both the world's messes and its marvels. Can't you see what you forfeit when your heart grows cold and hard? Consider if there's anyone you need to soften your gaze toward, someone you are shutting out, looking at disdainfully. Now shift your awareness to Me and My stance toward them. What do you notice?

Your Turn to Respond

❧ What word or phrase are you drawn to today and why?

❧ How does the reading relate to you and your life today?

❧ What would you like to say to God?

❧ What does God want to say to you? Listen.

DAY SEVENTY-EIGHT

And so I heartily recommended that you pursue joy,
for the best a person can do under the sun is to enjoy life.
Eat, drink, and be happy.
If this is your attitude, joy will carry you through
the toil every day that God gives you under the sun.
Ecclesiastes 8:15 (The Voice)

A Colloquy

What happened, My old friend? Life's vitality seems to have been completely drained out of you. I know life can often be hard. And at times, you add to its hardness when you forget that in spite of the overwhelming challenges you face, I have ultimately made you for life's pleasure and not self-inflicted pain. Sure, there will be pain over the years of your life, but the suffering that comes from your anxious toiling is not the point.

Have you forgotten, My friend, what brings you pleasure, what turns the corners of your mouth right side up? Could it be as simple as a piece of warm blueberry pie with vanilla ice cream melting on top? Or an ice-cold bottle of beer swirling down your throat after you've cut the grass on a steamy August afternoon? Don't deny yourself these simple pleasures. There won't be any skinny people in heaven!

But even better, learn to touch and be touched. Your skin can lead you to an endless discovery of new joys. Let your dog lick your face. Let the cool breeze caress your bare legs. The pleasure that can come from being touched will soothe your very soul if only you will let it.

So, learn to trust pleasure. Instead of being a slave to a strong work ethic, cultivate a growing, embodied pleasure ethic. You just might then begin to find the life you so deeply crave.

Have you ever considered your beliefs and assumptions about pleasure? Most people haven't. They just live out the same old scripts—messages that promote an endless cycle of guilt and shame. Whether you recognize this or not, what you've been taught about pleasure is woven deeply into every fiber of your being and informs everything. Will you let Me draw near to disarm all that still interferes with the gifts of your humanity?

Your Turn to Respond

❧ What word or phrase are you drawn to today and why?

❧ How does the reading relate to you and your life today?

❧ What would you like to say to God?

❧ What does God want to say to you? Listen.

DAY SEVENTY-NINE

When I applied myself to the study of wisdom and reflected on
the kinds of tasks that occupy people's attention on earth,
I noticed how little sleep they generally get, whether day or night.
I saw all the works and ways of God,
and it became clear to me that no one
is able to grasp fully this mystery called life.
Try as we might, we cannot discover what has been done under the sun.
Even if the wise claim to know, they really haven't discovered it.
Ecclesiastes 8:16-17 (The Voice)

A Colloquy

*I think you may be starting to get it, My old friend. There is a kind of wisdom that is
unwisdom yet is not unwise. Rather it is a deeper, older wisdom.*

*You observe, both in yourself and those around you, just how sleep deprived you've
become. Why, of all My beloved creatures, do you struggle with such a simple act?
Why is it so hard to receive this ancient, generous, and natural gift of Mine? Does it
remind you of your upcoming death, your all-too-soon departure?*

*Learn to sleep, old friend; learn from your beloved dog the fine art of napping. There is
a wakeful trust that allows your true nature to rest even when active. But there is also
a wakeful worry that always takes more than it gives, especially in the middle of the
night.*

*What will be, for the most part, will be. Even if you think you can fathom it, your life
and the way life works will always be more ancient, hidden, and deeper still. Give
your hands and your strength to the tasks at hand, but at the same time learn to give
your loving attention to My gentle presence. It is possible to repose while still awake,
but you cannot remain anxiously vigilant and make your descent into My golden
slumbers.*

*Take stock for a moment, My old friend. Do you notice an unnatural, anxious energy
or a hyper-vigilant drivenness that makes it difficult for you to receive the gift of rest?
Take some time to consider what that might reveal to you about where you are and
how you are.*

Your Turn to Respond

❖ What word or phrase are you drawn to today and why?

❖ How does the reading relate to you and your life today?

❖ What would you like to say to God?

❖ What does God want to say to you? Listen.

DAY EIGHTY

So I set my mind on all of this, examined it thoroughly,
and here's what I think: The righteous and the wise
and all their deeds are in God's hands.
Whether they are destined to be loved or hated, no one but God knows.
Everyone shares a common destiny—
the righteous and the wicked, the good [and the bad],
the clean and the unclean, those who sacrifice
and those who neglect the sacrifices.
The good and the faithful are treated no differently than the sinner.
Those who take an oath are treated no differently than those afraid to commit.
Such a great injustice!
Here is an evil that pervades all that is done under the sun:
the same destiny happens to us all.
Ecclesiastes 9:1-3a (The Voice)

A Colloquy

Destiny. Such a big, unfathomable word for you, My old friend. It troubles you so to fathom how the end will play out. When a life is finished the wise and the foolish, the wholesome and the wicked, the committed and the laissez faire all share one certain, common, universal conclusion. You think you'd prefer it if each one's destiny were guaranteed by their mastery of some existential formula. Would you like it better if I spelled out a detailed equation that makes life turn out as expected? Know this, try as you might, your final state, along with everyone else's, will never merely be the sum total of all your best efforts.

Why does this discourage you so? Have you even begun to consider the premise you hold to that you can ultimately determine how your life will turn out or how it will end? For that matter, what other assumptions do you unconsciously hold about life's fairness, about the world, about yourself, and especially about Me?

This common destiny is a common grace. Just as each of you is conceived and born into this world, you all cry out for help, for food, for security. So in the end you all return to be cradled in My arms, no matter what you've done between your first and last breath. Does this offend your sense of fairness, of justice? I hope not!

For just as a mother receives each child into her arms and onto her breast no matter the circumstances of her or his conception, so I stand more than ready to receive each of My children into My loving, eternal embrace. This homecoming is everyone's destiny! Can you be glad about that with Me? And don't forget, it is also your destiny, My beloved friend! Soon, very soon, you will come to know it for yourself so that you can then fully rejoice in our shared destiny. A destiny based on My new math, where both "one minus one" and "one plus one" in the end equal one.

What might happen around you today if you moved through the world fully embodying My grace? What if you didn't claim My grace only for yourself but actively envisioned and clearly detected My grace being poured out on all? I wonder how that would feel for you. I wonder how that would feel to others around you.

Your Turn to Respond

✦ What word or phrase are you drawn to today and why?

✦ How does the reading relate to you and your life today?

✦ What would you like to say to God?

✦ What does God want to say to you? Listen.

DAY EIGHTY-ONE

Human hearts are inclined toward evil;
madness runs deep throughout our lives.
And then what happens? We die. So long as we are alive, we have hope;
it is better to be a living dog, you see, than a dead lion.
At least the living know they will die; the dead don't know anything.
No future, no reward is awaiting them,
and one day they will be completely forgotten.
All of their love and hate and envy die with them;
then it is too late to share in the human struggle under the sun.
Ecclesiastes 9:3b-6 (The Voice)

A Colloquy

Now is still the day to live, My old friend. So live. Risk. Struggle. Love. Even fail while you still have time, while your heart still beats, and your lungs still draw in air.

I know you will make many, many mistakes in your lifetime. Practical mistakes. Moral mistakes. Relational mistakes. And spiritual mistakes. It seems as if both wrong-heartedness and wrong-headedness are deeply woven into the fibers of humanity's being. Don't be too hard on yourself or on others. I'm not.

I know that I've placed you in a difficult spot. At times, it can seem like an exit from this life would be the only relief available; to simply forget and be forgotten would seem to be the best arrangement.

Please, for My sake and for yours, don't check out prematurely. Whether outwardly or inwardly, stay the course; don't give up. Hold on to hope and stay engaged to the end. Love boldly. Hate with great discretion and restraint. And don't be afraid to follow desire and pleasure, but rather let your longings guide you up to the very end.

Your Turn to Respond

❧ What word or phrase are you drawn to today and why?

❧ How does the reading relate to you and your life today?

❧ What would you like to say to God?

❧ What does God want to say to you? Listen.

DAY EIGHTY-TWO

Seize life! Eat bread with gusto,
Drink wine with a robust heart.
Oh yes—God takes pleasure in your pleasure!
Dress festively every morning.
Don't skimp on colors and scarves.
Relish life with the spouse you love
each and every day of your precarious life.
Each day is God's gift. It's all you get in exchange
for the hard work of staying alive.
Make the most of each one!
Whatever turns up, grab it and do it. And heartily!
This is your last and only chance at it,
for there's neither work to do nor thoughts to think
in the company of the dead, where you're most certainly headed.
Ecclesiastes 9:7-10 (The Message)

A Colloquy

I'm so pleased, My old friend, that you finally seem to have gotten the message; that in reality, I am neither stingy nor hard on you. Your life is for living. So live the best you know how. Nothing could please Me more. Asceticism may be for a season, but life is a banquet. Eat up! Savor what's set before you. My communion with you is meant to be a feast of the senses.

And when you can—and hopefully it's often—wear the clothes you love—the way they look, the way they feel, the way they make you feel when you look in the mirror. Just to look at you makes My eyes sparkle. And don't just wait for special occasions to splash yourself with cologne. Treat yourself to your favorite scents.

But above all, cherish your beloved partner. It is she or he who will most abundantly complete the gift of your life. Be always an irrepressible, overflowing gift to one another. This is My richest blessing for you.

I know how hard you've worked all these years. I'm proud of you and commend you for all you've done for Me and for others. Don't deprive yourself up until the end. That's not My way. Don't end your days with increased toil and worries. Let go. Let yourself go. Learn to float easily into your life's conclusion. Consent as you would if you were carried by a gentle, loving river.

But now is the time to live your best life. Don't wait, because there will be an end, old friend. An end that leads to a new beginning, but an end, nonetheless.

Your Turn to Respond

✦ What word or phrase are you drawn to today and why?

✦ How does the reading relate to you and your life today?

✦ What would you like to say to God?

✦ What does God want to say to you? Listen.

DAY EIGHTY-THREE

I turned and witnessed something else under the sun:
the race does not always go to the swift,
the battle is not always won by the strong,
bread does not always fill the table of the wise,
wealth does not always accrue to the skillful,
and favor is not always granted to the knowledgeable;
but time and misfortune happen to them all.
A person can't possibly know when his time will come.
Like fish caught in a cruel net or birds trapped in a snare,
without warning the unexpected happens,
and people are caught up in an evil time.
Ecclesiastes 9:11-12 (The Voice)

A Colloquy

Have you noticed, My old friend, how there is both a seeming grace and anti-grace at work in the world? The grace of your remarkable and gifted capacities cut in half by forces and factors that thwart and stymie. As often as not, those who have been told they are the strongest or the fastest end up utterly undone and defeated. Or the ones who believe they are the most skillful and wise wind up disappointed and frustrated with how things turn out.

I have placed My deeper grace, a fierce grace, a grace that never feels like a gift within these apparent contradictions. It is a grace where a dynamic and living logic mysteriously frustrates even as it affects your healing and wholeness. Because it is often a disguised grace, who can know ahead of time what might happen there. You may even discover some new, life-giving stream that only flows from the jaws of life's worst catastrophes.

When will the coin fall? When will the other shoe drop, you often wonder? It's best for you to not know. For life is both a tragedy and a comedy. And it is often the unexpected events in life that call forth the purest tears of lament and the brightest bursts of joy.

Can you remember a past time or event when you had a sense of this? Probably not immediately or in the midst of it. I'm not fishing for a silver lining here. I understand how hard it was for you, but can you now see some gift or mercy that came to you from it, even though your pain and sorrow remains?

Your Turn to Respond

❧ What word or phrase are you drawn to today and why?

❧ How does the reading relate to you and your life today?

❧ What would you like to say to God?

❧ What does God want to say to you? Listen.

DAY EIGHTY-FOUR

One day as I was observing how wisdom fares on this earth,
I saw something that made me sit up and take notice.
There was a small town with only a few people in it.
A strong king came and mounted an attack,
building trenches and attack posts around it.
There was a poor but wise man in that town
whose wisdom saved the town,
but he was promptly forgotten.
(He was only a poor man, after all.)
All the same, I still say that wisdom is better than muscle,
even though the wise poor man was treated
with contempt and soon forgotten.
Ecclesiastes 9:13-16 (The Message)

A Colloquy

Don't despise your own anonymity, old friend. Over the years you have offered countless acts of service and grace-filled gifts that have been forgotten. Your life, as well as most of what you have done, will soon disappear from the memories of even those who love you best. Dissipating as an ephemeral and unsubstantial dream in the blink of an eye.

But I see. And even more, I deeply, deeply appreciate you and all you have meant to the world and to so many of My people.

I remember. And unlike all others, I will never, never forget. Did you know that I am grateful for you? Not in some general, diffused way. I'm grateful in a highly focused and particular manner. Take a moment to absorb this, My old friend. I am eternally grateful for you, and the many moments you brought real blessing into the world.

So, if you are forgotten—if others can't remember your name, or recall your face, or your deeds—remember this: I will hold your memory in My heart and laugh at the best and even the hardest times we've shared. Bravo, old friend. Bravo!

Is this a new thought for you: that I appreciate you, that I'm grateful for you, that I'm proud of you? How does that make you feel?

Your Turn to Respond

❧ What word or phrase are you drawn to today and why?

❧ How does the reading relate to you and your life today?

❧ What would you like to say to God?

❧ What does God want to say to you? Listen.

DAY EIGHTY-FIVE

The quiet words of the wise are more effective
than the ranting of a king of fools.
Wisdom is better than warheads,
but one hothead can ruin the good earth.
Dead flies in perfume make it stink,
and a little foolishness decomposes much wisdom.
Ecclesiastes 9:17-10:1 (The Message)

A Colloquy

Have you noticed, My old friend, how loud your preachers and your politicians have become? Never in the brief history of mankind has there been more machismo, more adulation of men—and sometimes women, but mostly men—who shout their hyper-aggressive rhetoric.

Can't you see it? Can't you feel what's happening? Somehow these self-appointed saviors turn everything and everyone into an existential threat. Fear in them (fear of losing power) unleashes a relentless flood of violent slurs and aggressive stances designed to mobilize My vulnerable ones to goose step to their raving madness.

All the while, My soft-spoken prophets, the ones who champion My love, the ones in step with My gentle ways seem to only whisper to the wind. Listen with the ears of your heart, My old friend; attend to the quiet depths of wisdom wherever you might find it. These kind souls, you will notice, offer no unsolicited advice. Rather they wait to weigh in. And when they do speak, please, slow down and take their words to heart.

Your Turn to Respond

✦ What word or phrase are you drawn to today and why?

✦ How does the reading relate to you and your life today?

✦ What would you like to say to God?

✦ What does God want to say to you? Listen.

DAY EIGHTY-SIX

Wise people move to the right
where they honor the goodness of God's creation,
while fools move to the left and choose to ignore it.
Ecclesiastes 10:2 (The Voice)

A Colloquy

You are always moving, My old friend. Everyone is. Just look around. Whether you recognize it or not, your movements come and go as certainly as the ebb and flow of the waves. Sometimes you move toward Me. I love to see you turning your face, your heart, your mind fully toward Me and life. I am always here waiting.

But sometimes you move in a thousand other directions. There are so many, many ways to move away from Me. Consciously or unconsciously, you can turn your back on Me; you can turn your eyes and ears in a direction that draws you away. I see it but can do little to stop the shifting and drifting. And so, I wait. Sometimes for a few moments, sometimes for a long, lonely time.

This movement back and forth seems troubling, foolish even, doesn't it? But it's the way you learn of My constancy—about My patience. And eventually, it is My hope, that your movement is consistently toward Me and toward life. Until then, I will keep waiting for your next return.

What do you notice about your recent movements, My old friend? Where are they taking you? Can you locate where you are today and name where you'd really like to be headed?

Your Turn to Respond

✦ What word or phrase are you drawn to today and why?

✦ How does the reading relate to you and your life today?

✦ What would you like to say to God?

✦ What does God want to say to you? Listen.

DAY EIGHTY-SEVEN

Fools are easily spotted when they walk down the street:
their lack of sense is obvious to everyone.
Ecclesiastes 10:3 (The Voice)

A Colloquy

You think you can so easily pick out those who are errant, don't you, My old friend? A lifetime of practice makes you quick to jump to conclusions about others. Without any effort you can size them up as they walk by and instantly know what they're all about. And unless they walk and talk like you, you immediately write them off.

Why is someone else the predominant focus of your judgment? Look in the mirror. Can you detect your own tomfoolery? Look in the mirror again, even with all your quirks and silly ways, can you see Me close behind you, My gentle hands on your shoulders, patient love in My gaze? Take in the whole picture. Then, go out and see with newly softened eyes the zigzagging ways of all My other children.

Your Turn to Respond

✤ What word or phrase are you drawn to today and why?

✤ How does the reading relate to you and your life today?

✤ What would you like to say to God?

✤ What does God want to say to you? Listen.

DAY EIGHTY-EIGHT

If someone in charge becomes angry at you,
don't leave your post;
a calm reply puts great offenses to rest.
Ecclesiastes 10:4 (The Voice)

A Colloquy

Both those who lead and those who follow will be given endless opportunities to develop character. And what is character, after all, but growing in likeness to Me? That's all. And that's enough, My old friend. The temptation you will face when you are in charge is to become frustrated, impatient, and unrealistic. As a result, you will lash out at those I've placed in your care. Remember, you are there to serve them, not be served by them.

On the other hand, when you are serving leaders who are immature or over their heads, the temptation will be to lash out in reaction to their trumped-up egos or simply throw in the towel and quit. There may be times to speak stern, direct words to those in positions of leadership. And there may be situations where it will be better to walk away and never come back. But before that, learn some restraint. Develop fidelity. And grow in compassion, even for those who misuse their positions and privileges.

Your Turn to Respond

+ What word or phrase are you drawn to today and why?

+ How does the reading relate to you and your life today?

+ What would you like to say to God?

+ What does God want to say to you? Listen.

DAY EIGHTY-NINE

Here's a piece of bad business I've seen on this earth,
an error that can be blamed on whoever is in charge:
Immaturity is given a place of prominence,
while maturity is made to take a backseat.
I've seen unproven upstarts riding in style,
while experienced veterans are put out to pasture.

Ecclesiastes 10:5-7 (The Message)

A Colloquy

Are you ever surprised that things run as well as they do, My old friend? When you consider the many complex decisions that those in power make, don't they often seem contrary to good sense or good practice?

How often have you witnessed this all-too-common scenario: those who are promoted in your organizations are those who have kissed and curried their way to undeserved favor with the powers that be. While others, who possess skillful talent and consistent character, are devalued and passed over. Haven't you contributed in your own way to this weakening of people's potential?

It is only by My quiet, sustaining grace and care for My people that these collective efforts do not fail completely. And sometimes, in spite of My attempts, they do crash and burn. Left to yourself, you, along with all your leaders will be drawn away and choose a self-serving scheme over My way of faithfulness and fruitfulness. That's why the pursuit of the common good is so uncommon in your culture. From now on, exercise good sense as well as good practice even if everyone around you is only concerned about their brand's appearance and their personal image.

Your Turn to Respond

❀ What word or phrase are you drawn to today and why?

❀ How does the reading relate to you and your life today?

❀ What would you like to say to God?

❀ What does God want to say to you? Listen.

DAY NINETY

If you dig a pit, you may fall into it.
If you tear down an old wall, a snake may come out and bite you.
Whoever quarries stones may be crushed by them,
and whoever splits wood may be hurt by flying debris.
If a tool is dull and no one sharpens its edge, the work will be harder;
the advantage of wisdom is this: it brings success.
If a snake bites before it is charmed,
there is no advantage in being a snake charmer.
The words of the wise bring them favor,
but those of the foolish endanger them.
Ecclesiastes 10:8-12 (The Voice)

A Colloquy

Wisdom does offer you a warning, My old friend. But not all warnings are rooted in My vision for you and the world. Though well-meaning, these small, self-protective warnings can cause you to retract, to never venture, to never try anything. For Mine is also a wisdom of risk! While many times the unexpected, even the undesirable, can and does occur when you attempt to move forward. Nevertheless, it is wiser to ignore the naysayers who sit in their pessimistic cynicism.

So do what you can to cooperate fully with reality. Be practical and prepare in ways that will (hopefully) lead to success. But never let the uncertainties or unknown dangers that may await you hold you back from attempting all that is in your heart. Come to Me and ask where to take a risk and where to play it safe. You're not alone in figuring this out, you know!

Your Turn to Respond

✤ What word or phrase are you drawn to today and why?

✤ How does the reading relate to you and your life today?

✤ What would you like to say to God?

✤ What does God want to say to you? Listen.

DAY NINETY-ONE

The talk of a fool self-destructs—
he starts out talking nonsense
and ends up spouting insanity and evil.
Fools talk way too much,
chattering stuff they know nothing about.
A decent day's work so fatigues fools
that they can't find their way back to town.
Ecclesiastes 10:13-15 (The Message)

A Colloquy

Don't be so quick to judge someone, My old friend, or diminish and write them off simply because they seem foolish in your eyes. Some, remember, have been limited by their genetic deficiencies or the deforming ways of their family, or even the culture's misguidedness that causes them to say or do childish things. These can lead to all kinds of destruction—it is true—but your cursing them and calling them out will only add to the tragedy of their lives.

Can you imagine how exhausting it must be for them to be limited in ways that you take for granted? Please, for My sake, for their sake, show a little compassion. You might just be surprised and gain a new sister or brother. The energy you expend in your judgments only wears you out. Compassion is free from all the name calling and labeling. Learn to be simple just as I am simple. Learn to simply see the one in front of you and remember that you do not know what life has been like for them. Then you will find that you can open your heart to both My babblers and blunderers.

Where do you notice yourself engaged in acts of name calling or labeling? How does that cause you to dismiss others? Take some time to consider how that is affecting your heart. Now, do you see more clearly who needs your compassion today?

Your Turn to Respond

❖ What word or phrase are you drawn to today and why?

❖ How does the reading relate to you and your life today?

❖ What would you like to say to God?

❖ What does God want to say to you? Listen.

DAY NINETY-TWO

Woe to the land whose king is a child
and whose princes start their feast in the morning.
Blessed is the land whose king is of noble heritage
and whose princes know when to feast,
who discipline themselves with strength and avoid drunkenness.
The roof sags over the head of lazybones;
the house leaks because of idle hands.
Ecclesiastes 10:16-18 (The Voice)

A Colloquy

If you think it will help, play out all the scenarios in your head. All that you observe may offer some instruction and help you find a better way. And you know how happy others are to promote their prized programs and strategies. But remember, My old friend, that these instructions are not universal precepts or principles. Though sometimes useful, they are never the same as receiving My personal guidance for you.

Believe it or not, I don't deal in universal generalities and precepts. I am fully present to what is and always content to engage with reality as I find it. For instance, using your example, if one child runs the show and his siblings are wasted by noon, I am there—not because it's what I want for them, but rather out of love and understanding.

Though I don't mechanically live out of some universal program or principle, I do pursue an enduring vision. A vision where you and I bless them and don't curse them. I know, and want you to know, that it can be a long and circuitous road that will heal all the brokenness of My beloved children. It's a highly relational process, an imperfect science that can never be reduced to simply following steps 1-2-3. Learn to be part of their restoration, even if it frustrates you. Instead of looking down your nose at them, remember the long road you've been on and where you started, My old friend.

Your Turn to Respond

❖ What word or phrase are you drawn to today and why?

❖ How does the reading relate to you and your life today?

❖ What would you like to say to God?

❖ What does God want to say to you? Listen.

DAY NINETY-THREE

A feast is made for laughter,
wine makes life merry,
and money is the answer for everything.
Do not revile the king even in your thoughts,
or curse the rich in your bedroom,
because a bird in the sky may carry your words,
and a bird on the wing may report what you say.
Ecclesiastes 10:19-20 (New International Version)

A Colloquy

Don't believe everything you read on a bumper sticker, especially when it's attributed to Me! Slogans and sloganeering can be fun. It can be useful too. But it can also be lazy, My old friend.

Let your own lived experience and our little conversations guide you. Let these inform what you believe, whether it's about joy or money or power.

Then, if you want, you can develop your own shorthand. But remember—there are no absolute and universal slogans to rely on except one. Love. When you open to Love and follow where Love leads you, you will find the richest fulfillment possible.

Are there any clichés you've adopted that, if you think about it, actually short-circuit your capacity to have your own first-person lived experience? Or perhaps you noticed that there are words you offer that, when shared, reduce another's life situation to something less than what it really is or what it could be?

Your Turn to Respond

✦ What word or phrase are you drawn to today and why?

✦ How does the reading relate to you and your life today?

✦ What would you like to say to God?

✦ What does God want to say to you? Listen.

DAY NINETY-FOUR

Send your grain across the seas,
and in time, profits will flow back to you.
But divide your investments among many places,
for you do not know what risks might lie ahead.
When clouds are heavy, the rains come down.
Whether a tree falls north or south, it stays where it falls.
Ecclesiastes 11:1-3 (New Living Translation)

A Colloquy

How can I explain this to you, My old friend? I have placed a vast array of networks into this dynamic world in which you live. Think for a moment of all the various and complex systems that are present: physical, botanical, biological, meteorological, astronomical, and even the mystery of quantum physics. Each of these, then, has a sub-order all of its own with increasing particularity and personality. In fact, there is a kind of order to the whole, and yet each system has a life and a center which is generally unconscious of its greater surroundings. A disordered order if you will.

That's why life is both wonderfully miraculous and maddeningly unpredictable. It's not Las Vegas, but there will be times when I will prompt you to place your means and assets on the line, gambling, as it seems, on a grand roulette wheel. And then, bingo! You win! You feel like you've hit the jackpot.

At other times I will urge you to play the conservative, to save a little here, squirrel away a little there. By now you know there will be stretches when all hell breaks loose and there will be neither planting nor reaping.

What I'm trying to tell you is that I don't want you locked into either extreme—always rolling the dice or always hoarding your cash to cover your bases. Ultimately the future is out of your hands. You can neither steer the wind nor predict when or where the giant tree might fall.

Remember that these other systems surrounding you aren't about you. They have a life and center of their own. So, while you learn to respect them, and get out of their way, don't avoid being touched by them, even if at times they scratch and bruise you. It's all part of the wobble I've left in My creation. Be nimble. Be bold. Be careful. Be generous. Be real and let all the others, both non-humans and humans, be real in their own way, too.

Your Turn to Respond

✦ What word or phrase are you drawn to today and why?

✦ How does the reading relate to you and your life today?

✦ What would you like to say to God?

✦ What does God want to say to you? Listen.

DAY NINETY-FIVE

Don't sit there watching the wind. Do your own work.
Don't stare at the clouds. Get on with your life.
Just as you'll never understand
the mystery of life forming in a pregnant woman,
so you'll never understand
the mystery at work in all that God does.
Go to work in the morning
and stick to it until evening without watching the clock.
You never know from moment to moment
how your work will turn out in the end.
Ecclesiastes 11:4-6 (The Message)

A Colloquy

Don't wait too long to discern what's in your heart or pursue it, My old friend. Always observing and weighing, worrying and calculating the angles will get you nowhere. Expect life to be a mystery. Accept it as it is. Don't try to get it all figured out before you finally do anything. As I said before, that will get you nowhere.

If you can't understand Me and My ways, why do you think you can fathom My creation? Creation bubbles, it wobbles, and sometimes it collaborates in surprising new ways. Take the risk to live, play, and work in My creation with Me. Take the risk to express yourself and be creative yourself! Who knows what might happen? But if you do nothing, or expend no effort, you can know for certain what will happen. Nothing.

Your Turn to Respond

✤ What word or phrase are you drawn to today and why?

✤ How does the reading relate to you and your life today?

✤ What would you like to say to God?

✤ What does God want to say to you? Listen.

DAY NINETY-SIX

Light is sweet; how pleasant to see a new day dawning.
Ecclesiastes 11:7 (New Living Translation)

A Colloquy

You love that star I've placed in the center of your solar system, don't you, My old friend? The one you call your sun—you need it. This small star is constantly bringing vitality to all aspects of your life, just as it is to every other earthling's life with whom you share this planet you call home.

Because of your unfailing relationship with your star, with its light and warmth, you are able to not just survive, but to joyfully thrive. No wonder the ancients tended to worship it. It is truly glorious and worthy of your wonder.

At night, when your star has disappeared, and you look up into the sky, at first you notice only that inky darkness which you call space. You think of space as empty, as void of anything of value. But it's not, is it?

As your naked eye acclimates, first you see one, then two, and soon a canopy of other lights. All of space above you seems to be cradling star upon star, planet upon planet, galaxy upon galaxy. So, too, My light is everywhere once your heart has begun to adjust to My spaciousness.

So look up. Look out. I am clothed in light, I am dancing in space, I am as far away as the most distant moon in the farthest spinning galaxy, and I am in the smallest strands of the DNA that make up your chocolate brown eyes.

And here's the truth within all of these wonders: you stagger Me! Can you really take that in? You stagger Me, just as much as you are staggered by it all. So together, let's be overjoyed and stagger, night and day, into the shimmering brightness.

Your Turn to Respond

◈ What word or phrase are you drawn to today and why?

◈ How does the reading relate to you and your life today?

◈ What would you like to say to God?

◈ What does God want to say to you? Listen.

DAY NINETY-SEVEN

If a person lives many years, then he should learn to enjoy each and every one;
but he should not forget the dark days ahead, for there will be plenty of them.
All that is to come—whether bright days or dark—is fleeting.
Ecclesiastes 11:8 (The Voice)

A Colloquy

*You rightly detect, My old friend, that your days, like the minutes, seem to grow swift,
sure legs and run quickly by. Fleeting, you call it. But try not to judge this passing of
time, the passing of your life, as a loss or something to regret. This shifting nature of
life is necessary, a gift really. It can cleanse your very being of the traumas you have
encountered. It can flood you with many beautiful, happy memories. It can carry you
forward into the answer to life's enduring question, "What's next?"*

*So let the hours, the days, the years wash over you. Don't try to hold onto them. To
do so is like trying to scoop the entire ocean into your two small hands. Enjoy each
day as often as you can. Endure the hard ones, no matter how many. And know for
certain that things will not always be as they are today. So be patient and ready to be
surprised once more by all that comes after.*

Your Turn to Respond

- What word or phrase are you drawn to today and why?

- How does the reading relate to you and your life today?

- What would you like to say to God?

- What does God want to say to you? Listen.

DAY NINETY-EIGHT

Be happy and celebrate all of the goodness of youth while you are young.
Cultivate a cheerful heart every day you have youth.
Go where your heart takes you. Take in the sights.
Enjoy, but remember that God will hold us accountable for all that we do.
When all is said and done, clear your mind of all its worries.
Free your body of all its troubles while you can,
for youth and the prime of life will soon vanish.
Ecclesiastes 11:9-10 (The Voice)

A Colloquy

I see it in your eyes, My old friend. You imagine that the best days of your life are past; that glory and joy belong to the young. That message is reinforced so often by your youth-obsessed culture. It's almost impossible to not let it seep in and color the way you see everything and everyone, including the way you look at yourself.

But here's what I want you to consider; your early years were just the beginning, a training ground to discover what brings you joy-filled satisfaction; an early experiment to find what your heart truly loves and how wonderful your life can be.

Realize, even now, that I'm holding you accountable. I'm not calling you out. I'm calling you in! I'm urging you on, not to diminish your pleasure and delight, but to increase it. My life-giving judgments are not a critique of your having lived too large, but for having lived too small. My appraisal of all that has come before is only intended to help you plumb the depths of My joy into your old age, and then beyond. So don't look back so wistfully. Look ahead to the adventures, even the soon-to-come adventure of descent and of death.

Your Turn to Respond

+ What word or phrase are you drawn to today and why?

+ How does the reading relate to you and your life today?

+ What would you like to say to God?

+ What does God want to say to you? Listen.

DAY NINETY-NINE

And so we come to the end of this musing over life.
My advice to you is to remember your Creator, God, while you are young:
before life gets hard and the injustice of old age comes upon you—
before the years arrive when pleasure feels far out of reach—
before the sun and light and the moon and stars fade to darkness
and before cloud-covered skies return after the rain.
Remember Him before the arms and legs
of the keeper of the house begin to tremble—
before the strong grow uneasy and bent over with age—
before toothless gums aren't able to chew food and eyes grow dim.
Remember Him before the doors are shut in the streets
and hearing fails and everyday sounds fade away—
before the slightest sound of a bird's chirp awakens the sleeping
but the song itself has fallen silent.
People will be afraid of falling from heights
and terrifying obstacles in the streets.
Realize that hair turns white like the blossoms on the almond tree,
one becomes slow and large like a gluttonous grasshopper,
and even caper berries no longer stimulate desire.
In the end, all must go to our eternal home
while there are mourners in the streets.
So before the silver cord is snapped and the golden bowl is shattered:
before the earthen jar is smashed at the spring
and the wheel at the well is broken—
before the dust returns to the earth that gave it
and the spirit-breath returns to God who breathed it,
let us remember our Creator.
Life is fleeting; it just slips through your fingers. All vanishes like mist.
Ecclesiastes 12:1-8 (The Voice)

A Colloquy

*I know, My old friend, that you are more aware of life's mortality than ever before.
You have seen much, experienced much, and endured much. As your years advance,
you may start to feel as if you are melting back into the earth, like an exquisite ice-
sculpture which can only resist the sun's heat for so long. Your aging is not a tragedy,
any more than the physics that returns the solidity of ice into flowing rivulets that*

again become water. I have made it so.

And now, here you are. You find yourself where your parents and grandparents were. You take up your place where all who have come before eventually have found themselves. You feel increasingly unsteady and weaker. It's more difficult to eat and digest your food or see and hear. Life seems to be shrinking, returning to a more basic, essential state.

With these losses and diminishments, also come real fears, real regrets, and more griefs. Besides that, you notice the disappearance of many longings and desires that once moved you. But your time is not yet here, My old friend. I am with you in all these changes, in all the unknown, unchosen paths that are now yours.

Do you remember your dream from many years ago? You had never imagined, nor seen an old Jesus, had you? But there He was, seated at an ancient banquet table, surrounded by old friends, like you are now. You watched them celebrating together with food and drink, as old women, dressed in bohemian fabrics danced with abandon in that small round room. You had entered by climbing a spiral staircase. And I watched you take it all in. Amazed. Our eyes meeting.

Soon, My old friend, you will join Me, your Old Friend, at this table. I am here, waiting for you, even now. Come further in, further up, and find your seat right next to Me.

Your Turn to Respond

❧ What word or phrase are you drawn to today and why?

❧ How does the reading relate to you and your life today?

❧ What would you like to say to God?

❧ What does God want to say to you? Listen.

DAY ONE HUNDRED

Not only did the teacher attain wisdom by careful observation,
study, and setting out many proverbs,
but he was also generous with his knowledge and eagerly shared it with people.
The teacher also searched for just the right words to bring hope and
encouragement,
and he wrote honestly about truth and the realities of life.
The words of the wise are like goads;
the collected sayings of the masters are like the nail-tipped sticks
used to drive the sheep, given by one Shepherd.
Ecclesiastes 12:9-14 (The Voice)

A Colloquy

My dear old friend, even though you are becoming hard of hearing, the ears of your heart are more open and clearer than they have ever been. You listen so well to what really matters. You hear My gentle whispers both within and without.

Thank you for noticing and cherishing My ways in the world, My ways with you. You have a great gift and you have not been idle with it. Even now you are exercising your aging energy in ways that bless others. In blessing them, you also bless Me.

Some whose ears are not as tuned to Me, can't yet hear as you do. They need your voice, your expressions. I am glad they have you to pass along your provocative images, ideas, and stories. My hope is that these will help My new friends open to Me and trust in My love as you have learned.

Don't be too hard on them. Remember how many wrong turns and missteps you have taken. And remember how I was always there; I never left you, even as I wept for you and the painful losses your choices produced. Remember the day I told you that My throne is a loveseat? Since it is Mine to do what I will, all My judgments have been for you, and never against you. I have cleared off the cushions. So come sit by Me and let us enjoy all that remains. Let us waste time together. Just sit for a while as we stare into the fire before us.

Your Turn to Respond

✦ What word or phrase are you drawn to today and why?

✦ How does the reading relate to you and your life today?

✦ What would you like to say to God?

✦ What does God want to say to you? Listen.

ACKNOWLEDGMENTS

This book began as a series of handwritten journal entries that I wrote in 2021-22. After the last entry was penned, I read some to Beth, my wife, to see if she felt they were worth publishing in one form or the other. She is forever my biggest cheerleader and the one who helps me see what a good idea is and what is not. I trust she was not entirely wrong in encouraging me to give shape to this present project. The book is much clearer, more readable, and user-friendly because of her editing eye. Her name should always be on the byline of everything I write!

Our good friend, Emma Hogsett, took the play on words "old souls" and ran with it, creating a warm, inviting cover that aptly conveys the invitation to take off your boots, sit down and enter into a leisurely three-way conversation.

There were countless times when Flo, our 14-month-old Springer-doodle, would sit at my feet, impatiently waiting for me to finish typing so we could go for a walk. On more than one occasion she would put her paw up on the keyboard and press until I had to stop. Hopefully not too many of her run-on sentences remain.

Finally, I'm grateful for the encouragement I received from Ignatius of Loyola, Eugene Peterson, Frank Laubach, Dorothy MacLean, Jim Wilder, and Vic Black. They each have modeled holy audacity in their own way as they sought to write in first person from the Voice of the Eternal!

FALL CREEK ABBEY
Renewing the Contemplative Spirit

Fall Creek Abbey is an urban retreat house in Indianapolis, thoughtfully designed for those seeking to reconnect their hearts with the heart of God. When someone walks through the doors into the Abbey, it's not uncommon for them to pause and want to name what they're feeling: the sensation of peace, quiet, welcome, and simple beauty. Many who come are seeking a sanctuary where they will be undisturbed and find rest in a setting that is supportive and nurturing.

"Our great joy at Fall Creek Abbey is to live a life that is right-sized for our season; one where small things are cherished, slowness is a virtue, and solitude is a welcome relief from a busy, noisy world."

This was a major theme when God prompted Beth and David to launch the Abbey in 2012 (formerly called Sustainable Faith Indy). As its hosts, they've currently welcomed over nine thousand guests to this still point in their city where individuals can step away from their responsibilities and reorient their heart to the loving heart of God.

As trained spiritual directors, Beth and David spend a good deal of their days sitting with women and men who want to hear God's voice of invitation and respond wholeheartedly. In addition, they speak regularly at workshops and conferences, design and facilitate group retreats, and lead the Fall Creek Abbey School of Spiritual Direction, where they train individuals in the art and ministry of spiritual companioning.

Beth and David co-authored When Faith Becomes Sight: Opening Your Eyes to God's Presence All Around You. Beth is the author of several other books, including Starting Something New: Spiritual Direction for your God Given Dream, in which she tells the story of Fall Creek Abbey. David has his MDiv from Trinity Evangelical Divinity School and, in addition to his other work, continues his private practice in career counseling with Direction 4 Life Work.

More information about Fall Creek Abbey and the Boorams can be found at FallCreekAbbey.org.

Made in the USA
Coppell, TX
31 March 2023